THE
DISCIPLE

THE DISCIPLE

ND Ekwegh

ISBN: Hardcover   978-1-5434-9271-2
               Softcover   978-1-5434-9270-5
               eBook   978-1-5434-9269-9

Print information available on the last page.

Scripture quotations marked NIV are taken from the *Holy Bible, New
International Version®. NIV®*. Copyright © 1973, 1978, 1984 by International
Bible Society. Used by permission of HYPERLINK "http://www.zondervan.
com/" Zondervan. All rights reserved. [HYPERLINK "http://www.biblica.com/
niv/" Biblica]

Rev. date: 12/12/2019

To order additional copies of this book, contact:
Xlibris
800-056-3182
www.Xlibrispublishing.co.uk
Orders@Xlibrispublishing.co.uk
785381

CONTENTS

1

Red or Blue Pill

(Luke 5:1–11)

Have you ever felt like you weren't good enough? Like you didn't belong? I definitely have. Whether in sports, relationships, or work, I struggle with that feeling every now and then. And if we are honest, the same is true for most of us in different aspects of life. There is always that voice in our ears whispering, 'You don't belong here' or 'You haven't got what it takes.'

Peter was just like us in that respect. When we first meet Peter, he isn't the cocky, mouthy chap we find later in the Gospels. He is a vulnerable man aware of his flaws.

As recorded in the book of Luke, Jesus preached to people while sitting in Peter's boat on the Sea of Galilee. When he finished, he turned to Peter and asked him to go out deep into the water and do some fishing. At this point, Peter must have thought, *Mate, you're a good preacher; I give you that. But you're no fisherman.*

Peter was probably in a particularly sensitive place at this time. Not only was he dealing with the depressing thought that he wasn't good enough as a man, but in addition to that, he was probably thinking he wasn't very good at his job either. They had worked hard all night with nothing to show for it. He made that point to Jesus, but out of respect, he decided to humour him by going. He expected no miracles at the end of it, just a blunt 'I told you so.'

Let's pause here for a second. Thinking about it, we sometimes respond to Jesus in the same way Peter did. His response to Jesus is one we can identify with. We think, *Yes, Lord, I know you say I shouldn't worry about anything. I know you say to have peace and to trust in your presence in my life. But Lord, you don't get it. I have tried. I have worked hard all night. I've worked at that marriage, that relationship, that job; I've worked hard at pursuing that dream and building that ministry. But it hasn't worked. I have worked hard on life, on being a better person, but I can't beat that habit or that addiction.* Like Peter, we want to give up. Yet we hear the voice of Jesus asking us to go again.

What if Peter hadn't gone?

If Peter hadn't paid attention when Jesus preached to the people, maybe he wouldn't have gone back to try again. Something about Jesus's message that day must have resonated with him, making him believe this man was worth giving a chance. But even at that, he could have gotten precious and allowed pride to prevent him from experiencing something really special.

The same is true for us. Sometimes we miss out on experiencing God doing something truly special in and through us either because of our pride or simply because we are not paying attention. When we stop paying attention to what God is saying to us, or when we allow pride to dictate our response to it, we hurt ourselves and the many others God intends to reach through us.

God is always reaching out to us, always making the first move. And he not only makes himself available but also makes himself vulnerable. He knows we may reject or ignore him, but he reaches out to us anyway. Even right now, God is reaching out to you. Are you listening? Are you humble?

The Bible says that God opposes the proud but gives grace to the humble (Proverbs 3:34; James 4:6). This is because it is impossible for God to work in and through hearts that are proud. Peter learns this truth first-hand as they sail back into the waters.

They went back where they failed and made a catch so big, their nets were not big enough to hold it. It was very much a 'my cup runneth over' moment. The catch was so sizeable that they needed the help of others to pull it in. How many times has God done that in our journeys? How many times has he brought success onto the set of our greatest failure?

When this happens, it feels like the scene in that Disney movie *Meet the Robinsons*. In the film, the young scientist Lewis has to return to the science fair, the scene of his latest failure, to receive the breakthrough moment that transforms not only his life but also the world he lives in. Lewis is initially reluctant to return; that place holds nothing but painful memories for him. But eventually he gets it. You must not be so afraid of failure that you don't even try.

Lewis had to return to the science fair, Moses had to return to Egypt, Jacob had to return home, Peter had to return to the deep waters; and you, where do you have to go back to? Where is the place God is calling you to that you want to give up on because things haven't gone as well as you would have hoped, because it carries painful memories of failure?

Whatever it may be, wherever it is, in faith you must go forth. What lies beyond is not something you want to miss.

Peter sees what happened, and putting two and two together, he realises this is no ordinary man standing in his presence. This is a special person. This is someone with the Spirit of God flowing through his veins. In the face of Jesus's strength, Peter becomes very aware of his own weakness. 'Go away from me, Lord; I am a sinful man!'

He is certain Jesus doesn't want to be hanging around his type. I meet a lot of people who feel that way. Even in my own journey, I feel like that every now and then. I get a strong sense that Jesus doesn't want a man like me, that he doesn't want someone with the flaws I have.

But that's where we are wrong. That's the exact someone Jesus wants to be close to. Luke revealed as much as he continued his biography on Jesus's life: 'By this time a lot of men and women of doubtful reputation were hanging around Jesus, listening intently' (Luke 15:1).

These were the people Jesus gathered around him, people like you and me with our 'doubtful' reputations. And here is why he chose such, because: you can only save people who recognise they need saving, and you can only help people who recognise they need help. As Jesus stated, 'I have not come to call the righteous, but the sinners' (Mark 2:17).

If we start to believe we are perfect and without flaws, that we've got it all figured out, we find ourselves drifting into dangerous territory, a place where we tell ourselves we don't need saving. It is dangerous because the one who doesn't need saving doesn't need a Saviour, and the one without need for a Saviour has no need for Jesus.

When we are in this place, following Jesus becomes problematic. Why follow someone we don't recognise a desperate need for, especially when he's calling us to places we'd rather not go? That sort of submission, which is the life of a disciple, only comes when we know and confess our deep and desperate need for Jesus. We place total faith and confidence in him because we recognise that without him, we are lost. That submission only comes when we are humble enough to admit we still need saving.

When, like Peter, we recognise our weaknesses, we receive God's amazing strength. When we recognise our imperfections, by grace we are empowered with the righteousness he gives.

Jesus did not reject Peter when the young fisherman confessed his flaws. In the same way, he didn't reject the Samaritan woman, the woman with the alabaster jar, the centurion, Zacchaeus, or anyone who came to him with their brokenness. He didn't tell Peter to go sort himself out and then find him when he was 'ready'. Instead, after Peter declared his unworthiness, Jesus said to him, and I'm paraphrasing here, 'Don't worry about it. From this point on, we are going to do great things together.'

And isn't this what he says to us every time we come to him in humility? Whether it is the first time we have accepted him into our lives or after our one hundredth sin, the message is still the same: 'Don't worry about it. From this point on, we are going to do great things together.'

Jesus is always giving us a new 'now,' a new beginning. God declares through Isaiah, 'Forget the former things; do not dwell on the past. See, I am doing a new thing' (Isaiah 43:18–19)! That message is as consistent and unchanging as our God. Forget the baggage; forget the old identity you had, the one that made you feel like you weren't good enough, that made you feel you didn't belong amongst the good and blessed, that had you shackled by sin and fear. Forget the former things. Don't dwell on the past. God is doing a new thing right now. And he wants you! Yes, you!

This is where we have a choice to make. It is like that scene in *The Matrix* between Morpheus and Neo. In that scene, Morpheus holds a red and blue pill before Neo and makes him the following offer:

> After this, there is no turning back. You take the blue pill—the story ends, you wake up in your bed and believe whatever you want to believe. You take the red pill—you stay in Wonderland, and I show you how deep the rabbit hole goes.

In that moment with Peter, Jesus makes the same offer. The Bible is full of people minding their own business before God steps in with an offer for them to mind his. It is an offer to put down a life that focuses on our own business and take up one that focuses on the business of God's kingdom, to swap being the main character in our own story for a supporting role in the story God is telling.

David was looking after his sheep when God showed up and anointed him as Israel's next king, Moses was ploughing through with a career as a shepherd when God appeared with an offer for him to lead the Israelites from Egypt. Matthew was busy collecting taxes when Jesus stepped in and asked him to come collect souls instead. Joseph was busy sleeping when God started filling his head with dreams. I could go on and on.

The Bible is full of God stepping in with a red or blue pill offer. It was the same for the people to whom he made the offer, it was the same for Peter, and it is the same for us: blue or red pill. The choice is either to give our lives to Jesus, wherever he may lead us, or hold on to our lives with its hopes and dreams for our own purposes.

Even after years of following Jesus, many of us are still sitting in front of Jesus, undecided about which pill to take. Others have taken the blue pill, having chosen to believe in something else rather than believe in him.

But our God is a gracious God, and whether you have swallowed the blue pill or are sitting there undecided, the offer remains. There is always a new now. As Jeremiah declared in Lamentations 3:22–23, 'The steadfast love of our God never ceases; His mercies never come to an end. They are new every morning; great is your faithfulness.'

So in this new morning, this new now, with God's love and mercies vibrant in Christ Jesus, let me put on my Ray-Ban shades, sit in Morpheus's chair, and make you an offer on behalf of our Lord. You can take the blue pill and close this book. The story ends, and you can carry on believing what you want to believe. Or you can take the red pill. Accept to follow Jesus on the journey of discipleship, and do great things together.

Over to you, Neo. I'd really love to show you just how deep the rabbit hole goes.

2

Who Do You Say I Am?

(Matthew 16:13–20)

People often have different perspectives about who Jesus is. He is perceived through different lenses, by non-Christians and Christians alike. I often wonder what my lens is. If Jesus asked me the same question he asked Peter, I wonder what genuine, honest answer I would give him. What would your answer be? What would be a true reflection of how you feel about Jesus?

The truth here lies in how we respond to him, because how we see him will always dictate what that response is. That was how it was for the Israelites all those years ago, and the same applies to us today. The disciples replied in verse 14, 'Some say John the Baptist, others say Elijah; and still others, Jeremiah or one of the prophets.' And we can dive even deeper into their psyches and maybe perhaps see ourselves in them.

I believe the different ways Jesus is perceived can be categorised into the following: as an entertainer, a threat, a means to an end, or an enforcer. We will explore each of them below:

Entertainer

For some, Jesus was no more than a guy who did impressive stuff. Earlier in Matthew 16, the Pharisees and Sadducees had come to Jesus demanding that he show them a sign from heaven. Some people only hung around Jesus in anticipation of what he might do next. Shortly after he fed the multitude, a group of people showed up again in anticipation of a bit more free grub. They even gave him hints: 'What sign will you give that we may believe you? What will you do? Our ancestors ate the manner in the wilderness' (John 6:30–31).

Even at his death Jesus couldn't escape people viewing him this way. Remember the man next to him on the cross? Even he demanded that Jesus pull out one of the tricks from up his sleeve to get them out of that jammy situation. This idea of Jesus is rife to many. He is simply 'a doer of great things'. And while this is part of who Jesus is, there is a whole lot more to him than that.

The problem with this perspective is that it assumes that Jesus exists only to satisfy our whims. He is a magician, an actor on stage, and we are the audience. His role is to impress us with a constant delivery of 'Look what I did!' while we marvel and shout, 'Encore! Encore!' But God's role is not that of a magician, and the role of a disciple is not that of an audience member. When we stumble into this mentality, it usually ends in disappointment.

Viewing Jesus this way often makes us reluctant to act until he does. We get stuck in a stand-off where we are waiting on him to 'show us what he's got'. We become like the Israelites, demanding he show us a sign so we can believe in him, and even suggesting the kind of sign that would grant him such a privilege.

But we are not alone in this. Even great men in the Bible, like Gideon, asked for a sign. And of the disciples, Thomas wasn't shy to request one either. His 'I will believe when I see' mantra earned him the title of 'doubting Thomas'. But we are often like Thomas and Gideon, aren't we? We are programmed to embrace the ideology that seeing is believing, and we refuse to move until God shows up visibly, or at least until we understand fully what the plan is.

I wonder, have you ever felt that way? Have you ever not followed up on something you felt led to do because you were waiting for God to do his bit first? Is there anyone brave enough to admit that, or am I the only dunce in the village?

A life lived following Jesus is a life lived in faith, as the writer of the book of Hebrews declared. No one can please God without faith, and faith, as someone once said, is taking the first step before God reveals the second.

Seeing Jesus as simply a 'doer of great things' limits our ability to follow him and know him completely. In this zone we are only in it for the good times. No relationship can function successfully that way. Jesus is not some gladiator, running around in our arena, killing wild animals and baddies, before looking up at us and shouting, 'Are you entertained?!'

Yes, he is strong and mighty. Yes, he moves the mountains and tames the storms. But he is a lot more than that. No one wants to be loved simply for what they can do. People want to be seen for who they are. Jesus wants you and me to see him, to really see him.

Threat

The Pharisees and Sadducees viewed Jesus as a threat, as someone who was going to make life difficult for them, someone who was going to change things drastically and in a way that they wouldn't enjoy. They loved their lives as they were and believed that the message Jesus represented was a threat to their way of life. As a result, they rebelled against him repeatedly, refusing to listen or respond, and in the end conspiring to kill him, to remove him completely from their story. Sound familiar? While it's easy to tut-tut at the religious leaders, there are still many in our world today who see Jesus as a threat. And yes, that includes you and me.

Sometimes we see him as a threat to living a particular way, a way that we believe brings us enjoyment. We think following Jesus may suck all the joy out of our lives. And even when we manage to get past that hurdle, we are confronted with the burdensome reality that many times, God's plans and dreams are very different from ours—and we like ours. Ours are well thought out and lead to a happy ending; God's, however, seem not carefully considered at best.

We want to go one way, but he's calling us in another direction, one that doesn't look particularly appealing—and we don't like it. Like Jonah we want to go to Spain, but God is calling us to Nineveh via whale belly. Like Moses, we're drifting into retirement, when God chooses a new career for us in leading difficult people. Like the Pharisees, we are comfortable in our interpretation of the gospel and with our church pews, and then Jesus shows up with a new interpretation that is completely foreign to everything we've held true.

God sometimes seems to want something different from what we want, and that leaves us a bit unconvinced and fearful of his intentions.

But as John declared in 1 John 4:18, perfect love drives out fear. Once we understand that God's love for us is perfect, we understand there is no need to be afraid of him or what he might do. We need not fear the intentions of someone who did not think of his own well-being but gave himself completely to save us, suffering the worst kind of torment and making the biggest of sacrifices. This is a Saviour who is always working for our good.

Sometimes there is this misconception that God is only looking out for number one, that he is only interested in *his glory*. That's all it's about. He doesn't care about what we want; he just cares about *his glory*. It is something that we unconsciously champion as leaders. But the misconception lies in not fully understanding what God's glory is.

Ultimately, above all else, God is a Father, and like any good parent his greatest pride is in seeing his children thriving, becoming the best that they can be. Peter declares in 1 Peter 2:9–10 that we are God's treasures. Paul adds to that in Ephesians 2, where he says we are God's masterpiece. Bottom line: we matter to God, and his strongest desire is to see us doing well. This is why he was prepared to come to die for us, because God will do whatever it takes to help us, as any good parent would do for his or her child. Seeing his children thrive, seeing them fulfil their potential, that is what he takes pride in. This, I believe, is where his glory lies. Jesus shared as much when he spoke of the great rejoicing that takes place when a sinner finds his or her way home. God's greatest desire is that we make it home.

So, yes, it is true that God drives the path of our lives for his glory, but his glory is very much in our best interests. It is very much with our well-being in mind. And what is the key to seeing this glory? Paul alludes to this in Colossians 1:27: 'Christ in you—the hope of glory.' It is our connection with Jesus that gives us the best chance of experiencing the best life. He is the key to a great life, rather than a threat.

Means to an End

Similar to seeing him as an entertainer is our tendency to see Jesus as a means to an end, some sort of get-rich-quick scheme. That's definitely the way Judas saw him. For Judas, Jesus was a ride to the top, a man whose wisdom and popularity was going to make him wealthy. And Judas planned to ride the wave of Christ's success to the very end. But then Jesus wasn't behaving as he expected him to. This was a man who had the knowledge of not just where to cast nets for fish but also which fish had coin in them (Matthew 17:27). This was a man who could feed multitudes from a little, a man who could do things that were beyond belief. Yet Judas's pockets were not getting as fat as he would have hoped. It got too much for him, and in the end, he decided to get rich via Jesus in a different way.

It was a decision he was unable to live with. Eventually he resorted to taking his own life.

It's easy to criticise Judas, but do we not make the same mistake? Sometimes we see Jesus as a shortcut to life. A man who helps us dodge the long roads of life's struggle. And when it doesn't work out that way, when things aren't as smooth or as quick as we have hoped and prayed, like Judas we begin to get itchy feet. Those itchy feet lead us to accept the thirty pieces of silver; an affair, alcohol, retail, addiction, work, or whatever else comes up as an alternative. We turn to someone or something else, just as Judas Iscariot did.

Judas got tired of waiting for Jesus. He hadn't signed up to wait. He knew exactly what Jesus was capable of, and he couldn't understand why he was faffing about. Judas was done with playing the patience game; he wanted success *now*.

Someone once opined that one of the main problems we have today is a lack of patience. We want everything now. We want sex now! We want food now! We want success, power, and status now! So, rather than build and work and grow, we look for shortcuts to get there immediately. But then we find ourselves like Judas, unsatisfied with our thirty pieces of silver. How many good lives have been lost to silver because the thirty pieces did not deliver on what they promised?

We traded a journey with Jesus for a quick payout because he moved too slowly for our liking. But that quick payout does not give us peace, does not give us hope, does not pick us up when we fall, and doesn't fill us with a love that makes us feel valued and whole. It does not fill us with words that bring us life. Only Jesus does that. Only Jesus *can* do that.

Judas realised this for himself, but by the time he did so, it was too late; he had gone too far. Let us walk away from the house of the chief priests lest we make the same mistake he did. Their silver may be shiny, but it is poison and will never deliver on what it promises.

Enforcer

Lastly, another misconception is when we see Jesus as an enforcer, some sort of Judge Dredd character. For a long time this was what the disciples believed about Jesus. They may have jumped on the bandwagon after having seen him chase the corrupt layabouts out of the temple and assumed this was what it was all about, a strong desire to be right, to win arguments rather than win souls.

To be fair, we can all be like that to varying degrees. Met with a hostile reception from a Samaritan village, the disciples asked Jesus whether they should call down fire from heaven to destroy the villagers (Luke 9:51–56). Jesus was not impressed.

In today's church too much time can be spent calling down fire from heaven, calling it down on all those who are different in behaviour or beliefs. Let me let you in on a little secret: fire is not going to come.

The disciples mistook Jesus for Barabbas, an insurrectionary who used violence to impose his views on those who represented something different. They expected Jesus to eventually lead a charge against the Romans and establish his kingdom on earth this way, giving them high-ranking status as fellow 'enforcers'. But it wasn't just the disciples. Most of Israel expected the Messiah to be that kind of figure, someone with the mystical powers of Samson or the battle-hardened hands of David, perhaps with the fire of Elijah, or perhaps a rod-wielding plague dispenser like Moses. But the kind of kingdom Jesus was coming to establish, and the way he was choosing to establish it, was very different.

I've met many who believe that to disciple is to dictate to others how to live their lives, to be crude, hard, and deliver a modern-day version of the Ten Commandments. But if we are true disciples of Jesus, we should disciple others in the way he discipled us. And how did Jesus disciple us? By laying down his life for us, all of us, even for the Pharisees, whom he saved his strictest words for. Even for them he said, 'Father, forgive them. They know not what they do.'

The idea of Jesus as an enforcer is one that cripples us as church. It cripples our ability to make disciples, which is the number one function. The job of a disciple after all is to make other disciples through one's gifts, talents, abilities, personality, and stories, but ultimately through a heart of love and grace.

God's cry to humankind has not changed from what he said to Adam in the Garden of Eden. He is still saying to us, 'Be fruitful and multiply.'

We are called to be light of the world and salt of the earth (Matthew 5:14–16) in the same way Jesus was for us, as he shone his light into our lives and took away the bitter taste of sin from our mouths. A failure to see Jesus as our Light and Salt, as the man who put us right rather than the man who wanted to be right, completely misplaces our priority and our identity. For too long the church has been lost in trying to win an argument, rather than working to make all people right with themselves and ultimately with their God.

So who do you say Jesus is? Under the inspiration of the Spirit, Peter declared that Jesus was the Messiah, the Son of God. In making that declaration, he was stating that Jesus is Lord of all. The words 'Jesus is Lord' may roll off the tongue easily, but if he is, then that implies complete surrender on our path—surrender to his will, his ways, and his love. And that is something that we struggle with. We don't like the word *surrender* or *submit*. Many strike out the word *obey* from the traditional marriage vows for that very reason. At the end of our time, we want to be able, like Frank Sinatra, to boom out the words 'I did it my way!'

But a life with Jesus as Lord means that that famous song can never define our journey. Ours is one of submission and surrender to the will of our Lord Jesus Christ. This is the calling of a disciple. Paul lets us in on why this should not be as hard to do as it sounds. When he admonishes husbands to love their wives, he uses Christ as an example (Ephesians 5:25). Love your wives as Christ loved the church and gave up himself for it. We need have no fear of one who loved us so much that he was willing to die for us.

Think about it for a minute. Say you know someone at work who is wiser than you and has more knowledge and experience of how things work, someone who has information and insight that you are not privy to, someone who is a genius at what he or she does and, to top it up, is completely committed to your success. Would you not listen to this person? Would you not follow this their lead and submit to their counsel?

I most definitely would. It would be unwise to do otherwise, wouldn't it?

3

Are You Sitting Comfortably?

(Matthew 14:22–31)

I remember learning to swim. I must have been about eight or nine years old, and I was causing my coach a lot of frustration. His instruction was simple: I was to swim vertically from one end of the pool to the other. But I didn't fancy being underneath the water for that long. So every time I set out, I would swim for half the lap and walk for the remainder of it. We were at the shallow end of the pool, so this was easily done. The coach tried to encourage me each time to try to swim to the end. He was convinced I could do it, but I wasn't. Each time he set me off, I would do the same thing, until he was completely exasperated. He picked me up, took me to the deep end of the pool, and chucked me in the water. Suffice to say I swam right to the end this time around, like a fish on steroids, hitting record time in the process.

Now, I doubt that technique came from the verified handbook of how to teach a kid to swim, but even if not quite as dramatic, we've all been on the learning curve in some shape or form. Take learning to ride a bicycle for instance. We start off maybe with some stabilisers, but then the point comes when we have to learn to ride the bicycle without the stabilisers on.

We have to confront our fear of falling, confront the possibility that we may fall. It is the same with learning to ice skate. At some point we have to leave the barriers, go for it, and confront that fear head-on. At the first few attempts, most of us fail. We fall off the bike, or crash our bums on the ice, but it's all part of the process of getting good at something. It's all part of growing up.

In Paul's first letter to the church in Corinth, he speaks about how he gave them milk, not solid food, because they were not ready (1 Corinthians 3:2), and later, in chapter 13, he talks about how when he was a child, he reasoned like a child, but the time came when he had to grow up and put childish ways behind him.

The time came when he had to take the stabilisers off the bicycle, to swim to the end of the pool without stopping. The time came for progression, for growing up.

It's normal to want to see progression in our lives and in the lives of those we love. We cheer when a baby sits up for the first time or takes his or her first steps. We cheer at potty training and dry nappies. It's exciting because they are progressing; they are becoming who they should be at that stage of their lives. And when things aren't quite progressing as we believe they should be, we worry. We get anxious.

The desire to see our children progress and move forward in life is similar to the desire God has for us. He too wants us to progress, to become ourselves. God has made each of us as unique individuals. And in each of us, he has invested specific qualities to enable us fulfil his purpose of being light and salt to our world. As we grow from stabilisers to two-wheelers, getting more and more comfortable in our skin, we become those people, and the world is a better place for it.

One of my favourite verses in the Bible comes from Job 37:5–6: 'God's voice thunders in marvellous ways; he does things beyond our understanding.

He says to the snow, "Fall on the earth," and to the rain shower, "Be a mighty downpour."'

In other words, God says to the rain, 'Be rain,' and to the snow, 'Be snow.' And he says to you and me, 'Be you.' God doesn't call us to give what we don't have, and he doesn't call us to be somebody else; his vision is for us to grow, develop, and discover who we are.

Leo Buscaglia has that famous sentiment: 'Your talent is God's gift to you. What we do with it is our gift back to God.'

There is a lot in us to discover and unwrap. It is like Christmas Day with presents wrapped under the tree. You want the gifts you've bought to be unwrapped, and you want them to be used. What if they are never unwrapped or used? If that jumper is never worn and that toy never played with, it breaks your heart, doesn't it? Especially if you invested in that gift, believing it would make the recipient happy, that it would make his or her life more complete.

The same is true for the gifts that God places within us. He wants them to be unwrapped, and he wants them to be used. He placed these gifts in our lives not as a burden, but to enrich us and make us more complete.

Jesus leads the way in showing us how to use the gifts that God has placed within us. While he walked on earth, he used all that he had and that came into his space to bring healing to the world. We are called to do the same, to discover the gifts that God has placed within us, and to use them to enrich our world.

There is one problem, though: the boat.

The boat represents our comfort zone—our stabilisers and our shallow end, the things that serve as a substitute for faith. We harbour the fear that we will fail and land flat on our backsides, and so we play it 'safe'. But playing it safe never saved anyone. Playing it safe never enriched any lives. And the very definition of being a disciple of Jesus means we don't get to play it safe. It is not an option to be considered.

You see, the key to discovering who we are, the key to growing up as disciples, is stepping out of our comfort zone and taking that step of faith. In the passage from Matthew 14 where Peter walks on water, we find that when the disciples initially see Jesus, their first reaction is fear. And many times for us, when Jesus initially shows up on our horizon, our initial reaction is fear. It is a common denominator.

Take Moses for example. God was calling him to go and lead his people, and Moses was afraid of public speaking. Besides, the last time he tried to 'lead', he ended up being wanted for murder. Jacob was nervous about going back home because it meant facing his brother Esau, whom he had wronged. Abraham, too, was afraid when he followed God's call to leave his land and go travelling, so afraid that on occasions he asked his wife, Sarah, to pretend to be his sister. And the first disciples were scared several times, but they still moved forward. Some took persuading, but they all took that step forward in faith.

Many times when God shows up on our scene and calls us in a particular direction, it is scary. But he recognises this and reassures us. In verse 27 we see Jesus *immediately* reassuring the disciples: 'Take courage! It is I. Don't be afraid.'

God chooses similar words to speak to Joshua as the latter faces the daunting task of filling Moses's shoes: 'Have I not commanded you? Be strong and courageous. Do not be afraid; do not be discouraged, for the Lord your God will be with you wherever you go' (Joshua 1:9).

God is amazing in that he doesn't judge us or get exasperated with us. He understands that we are afraid, and he understands why we have reservations. And so what does he do? He moves quickly to reassure us.

Like he said to Joshua, he says to us, 'Have I not commanded you?' In other words, *It is I who has told you to step out of your comfort zone; you can trust me.*

We need not fear when it is God who has called us.

Going by that logic, it makes sense to discern that it is God who is calling us forward. Peter doesn't just go ambling out of the boat like a drunk sailor. He asks Jesus, 'Lord, if it's you, tell me to come to you on the water.'

It is important to spend time seeking God's face and his will. Part of growing up in faith is learning at the feet of our Saviour, taking time out to actually listen to him lead. Sometimes we don't do this because we are afraid of what he may say, and other times we fill up our lives with so much noise that we are not even asking the question, let alone receiving an answer.

So, when last did you make yourself available to God?

Because when you do, the likelihood is that he is going to challenge you to get out of the boat, to leave milk and begin to try out solids, to become yourself. Jesus touches on this in the parable of the talents, which you can find in Matthew 25:14–30. There were those who took the talents their master had given them and went and did something with them, and then there was the one who allowed the fear of failure to hold him back. This man buried his talents instead and returned them to his master unused.

Jesus is clear about what he wants us to do with the gifts he has given us: he wants them to shine like light. As we touched on earlier, this is how God is glorified, when we thrive as ourselves.

Jesus makes the point that no one has a light and hides it (Matthew 5:15). To him, we are light, so he doesn't want to hide us. He wants us out there, not crouched down in some boat. And he expects us to do something with the gifts we've been given, to make them shine. But sometimes we are like the servant who hides his talent. We are reluctant to step out of our boat because we are afraid of failing. We know that we can't dictate to God how he handles the particular journey we are on, and we know that we can't dictate to him what success looks like or when it would occur. And while we feel a prompting of God's voice, many times we are working with limited information as to what the plan is and where exactly God is going with this.

And so, especially if we've suffered disappointment in the past, we take the easy option: we do nothing. We just sit still in the boat and wait to get to the other side.

The problem with that approach is this: the gifts and talents that are activated by our walk of faith are the answer to someone's prayers. Whenever we hide rather than shine, there is someone somewhere who is worse off as a result. There is a part of the world that remains dark because our light is not shining, and there is a life that remains bitter because our salt is not flavoursome. When we hide, it is not just we who miss out.

This is perhaps why the master's reply is pretty harsh in the parable. Not only has the servant gotten a misconstrued impression of who his master is, but also by refusing to take a chance, he has inadvertently denied others of the particular kind of healing only he can give. Because you are unique. No one can worship God the way you can, and no one can give God glory the way you can. If you don't become you, there is no one else. Another you simply does not exist.

In the story preceding that of Jesus walking on water, we learn about how Jesus fed the five thousand, and this story is very apropos in the context of our discussion. There was a boy with only five loaves of bread and two fish amidst a multitude of people who needed feeding, five thousand men, not counting women and children. From where the disciples were standing, this was a hopeless situation. But nothing is hopeless when Jesus gets involved.

Like the disciples, we are sometimes disheartened by the size of the task at hand or the obstacles in our way. Sometimes I look at the suffering and injustice in the world and I want to throw in the towel. I lift up my eyes to the heavens and say, 'Lord, just come back. I don't know that the world can take any more of this torture.'

But Jesus has not given up on the world, and he hasn't given up on his church. And if, rather than feeling despair at the size of the task at hand, we were to place what we have in the hands of our Saviour, we would see just what he's capable of. If we refuse to give in to our fears, if we refuse to allow them to keep us crippled in the boat, and if we instead take the step of faith just like Peter did, then we too will walk on water. We too will see God bringing healing to our world in ways we may have been previously unable to imagine. And even better, we will get to know the absolute thrill of him doing that work through us.

But here's the thing, and there's always a thing: One of the mistakes we make, that I certainly have made, is believing that once we hear Jesus and we step out of the boat, everything will fall into place immediately. And when things don't, when there are obstacles and hindrances, when it gets tough and we begin to sink, we are left questioning everything. It is why many often go back to the boat if they can, or at least keep an eye on it. When Peter stepped out, he began to walk on water, just as his Lord was doing, but then he felt the strength of the wind and the crash of the waves, and he got scared and began to sink.

Do you feel the waves right now? Do you feel the strong breath of the wind? Are you sinking?

We've all been there. We took the step of faith, but now failure seems more likely than success. When God sent Moses to Pharaoh, with every request to let the people go, Pharaoh made life more difficult for the Israelites under his charge. I bet that made Moses popular. And what about the Israelites journeying to the Promised Land? After travelling for a long time in the wilderness, they begin to long to for Egypt. Why? Because it was a place they knew. The wilderness was an unknown, a vast mass of nothing, whereas Egypt was their boat. And boats can take on different shapes and forms: a relationship, a job, a habit or lifestyle, even a church. And when the road gets tough and we see the waves, the easy option sometimes is to quit and return to the boat. But the Bible is filled with stories of those who kept going even when the road got tough.

David kept going even when the road to the throne of Israel was diverted towards the stormy waters of life as a fugitive, Joseph kept going even when his path was rerouted to prison, as was Paul's. Moses carried on demanding that Pharaoh let God's people go, and Abraham kept trusting in God's promise to make him a father of nations. We all know how those stories ended: with David on the throne, with Joseph saving not only his family but also several nations, with the Israelites in the Promised Land, and with the birth of Isaac, Israel, and us.

What God did in those stories, he will also do in ours. The one who calls us is faithful.

There will be some opposition, because as Jesus teaches in the parable of the weeds (Matthew 13:24–43), when he plants his people around the world to carry the message of the kingdom, to be light and salt, rain and snow, there is also another one who is planting. The enemy is planting weeds, trying to get in the way of the work God is doing in our world. But fear not: God does not fail, and he is always with us. And because he is with us, this story ends well. It may not go in the direction we think it will, but it ends well all the same. Joseph ended up in prison, but being in prison was key to him becoming himself and healing his world in the process. Without prison he may not have discovered the gift of interpreting dreams, and without that discovery he would not have had the tools to fulfil his calling. Without the wilderness experience, David would not have honed his leadership skills or penned those psalms that still bless us today. And Paul ending up in a prison cell meant he had to write rather than visit the churches, and hence we have a record of his Holy Spirit–inspired words of wisdom.

Joseph, as did David and Paul, discovered that what may have been intended to harm them, God used to propel them to where they needed to be. And he will do the same in our lives. The setbacks and discouragements, the hurts and disappointments—God can and will use them to propel us forward.

On our part, we need to constantly remind ourselves to keep our eyes on Jesus and not on the storms, to keep our eyes fixed on his loving gaze, our ears tuned to his words of encouragement, and our hearts connected to his. The lyrics of that great hymn tell us this:

> Turn your eyes upon Jesus,
> Look full in his wonderful face,
> And the things of earth will grow strangely dim
> In the light of his glory and grace.

And when we turn our eyes to him, we realise, as Peter did, that he is always with us. When Peter began to sink, he cried out to Jesus to save him. Verse 31 tells us that Jesus again *immediately* reached out his hand and caught him. In other words, Jesus was right next to Peter all that time; he need not have worried or been afraid. There was no way Jesus was going to let him sink under the waves. There was no way Jesus was going to let the story end in failure. If Peter had only kept his eyes on his Lord, he would have seen that there was nothing to fear.

So, where are you in this story?

Are you sitting in the boat? Then step out in faith.

As Mark Batterson writes in his book *Chase the Lion*, 'Sometimes you have to chase a dream that's destined to fail without divine intervention.' Sometimes you just have to get out of the boat. No disciple of Jesus can remain in the boat and truly discover themselves. It was a lesson Peter learnt that night.

And if you have stepped out, or are preparing to do so, do not be afraid; keep your eyes on your Saviour, and hear these words for all your todays and tomorrows: 'I am the Lord your God who takes hold of your right hand and says to you, Do not fear; I will help you' (Isaiah 41:13).

4

You Do Not Want to Leave Too, Do You?

(John 6:60–69)

'From this time many of his disciples turned back and no longer followed him.'

Verse sixty-six of the sixth chapter of John's gospel is a chilling one. Jesus had just been teaching in the synagogue in Capernaum, but the feedback wasn't great. If you've ever had negative feedback on a sermon you've preached or a talk you've given, you know what that feels like.

The Bible is not half wrong when it talks about Jesus understanding what it's like to be us.

Jesus had just preached a sermon, one he believed in, one he hoped would bring life to those who listened. But what was the response? Rejection. Even a good number of people who had initially chosen to put their faith in him decided he was not worth following anymore. They found his message too hard to listen to and too difficult to accept. It didn't agree with them, and so they walked.

What would make you walk? What would make you stop following?

For Jonah it was a call to go to Nineveh. He couldn't overcome his prejudice against the people who lived there, and so he ran from God. For David it was a beautiful woman having a shower. For the rich man, it was his status. For Judas it was his love of money. What is the step too far for you? What is the biggest source of conflict that kicks against the influence of Jesus over your life?

In one of Jesus's parables, the one about the banquet, the host sends out invitations inviting several guests to join him for a great feast. He is, however, disappointed to learn that his invitations are not accepted. The guests send their apologies. Different things are going on which prevent them from attending the feast, ranging from business commitments, to relationships, to possessions that need 'trying out'. In other words, they had prior commitments that they just wouldn't give up.

What are we doing with our invitation to the feast?

Do we have prior commitments that following Jesus would get in the way of? Do we have a dream we want to chase, a position we aspire to, or a possession we must have?

In the passage we read earlier, Jesus had just given a sermon about an invitation to a feast, only it wasn't the kind of feast the people wanted. They came asking for a miracle so that, in their own words, they 'may believe in him', but Jesus's response was to tell them that the only thing they needed was his Word and his sacrifice. That was not enough for them. They wanted something tangible, like the manna that their ancestors received.

And sometimes we carry the belief that the evidence of a complete life is found in things that can be seen.

As for Jesus's disciples, they wanted him to give in to the desires of the people. If all it took were a few bread buns dropping from heaven, then he might as well do it; they knew he was capable. Not too long ago he had not only fed a multitude from little but also had walked on water. Jesus, though, points to faith, to the unseen, indicating that the key to eternal life is trusting in who God is.

Somewhere along the line, the message is lost, and in between arguing about the merits of cannibalism and undermining Jesus as simply 'Jo and Mary's boy', the people, and many of his disciples, decide to look for an alternative option to finding completeness in life.

They choose to look for another Lord to follow—and in this life, there are many alternatives.

Many 'lords' compete for the summit position in our lives, offering their own brand of eternal life. And the offer that these lords make always appear more attractive than the one our Saviour holds out. Jesus was very honest about this when he spoke about the narrow and wide gates in Matthew 7:13–14. The alternative always looks more attractive.

There's a reason it's called temptation—it's tempting.

For Jonah, Spain seemed a lot more appealing than Nineveh. David found the sight of Bathsheba's naked body more desirable than the sight of war. For Eve, the option of being God sounded a lot better than following God. These are just a few examples of the attractive propositions that come our way from these other lords. We are bombarded on an almost day-to-day basis. The volume of the world is turned up, and it's all we can do to turn it down let alone drown it out completely. Thankfully, in Jesus, we have someone who understands our struggles. He himself was offered alternatives by the enemy, but he stood firm. And in him we can stand firm too.

Jesus goes to the wilderness to fast and pray before the start of his ministry, and at the end of forty days of fasting, the enemy shows up to tempt him (Matthew 4). Just like the enemy does for us, he surrounded Jesus with temptations. These temptations, when presented to us, give us a different message to believe in and a different god to put our faith in. The first thing the enemy does in Jesus's case is to highlight that what he needs is not present. Jesus needs bread, but he is surrounded by stones.

And doesn't Satan love to point at our stones?

The Devil ascertains that these stones turning to bread would affirm who Jesus is as God's Son. They would be the evidence that God is with him. Satan knows Jesus is hungry after a long fasting period. He can sense his vulnerability, and so he goes for it. He tries to get Jesus to base his faith on what he can see, on the tangible.

And the enemy does the same in his dealings with us. He points to the presence of bread as validation of who we are, and by the same logic, he points to its absence as a reason to doubt. If you are God's child, if God is with you, then there will be bread. The job will work out, the relationship will be smooth, all your dreams will come true, etc. In telling us these things, the Devil attempts to get us to take our comfort and build our hope on material and tangible things, rather than in and on God.

Satan tries to point to the absence of bread and the presence of stones as evidence of God's absence on our journey.

'If you are God's child, turn these stones into bread.'

Too many times we get suckered into this mentality. Like Thomas, we'll believe when we see it. We want to dig our hands into Jesus's side and palms before we'll trust he's there. It's easy to give into depression and worry, because there isn't a big sign to declare God's presence. Rather, everywhere we look, we see stones: the worrying bank balance, the mounting bills, the doctors' appointments, and other disappointments. We want bread, but we see stones everywhere.

Earlier on, when we looked at Peter walking on water, we saw how he got distracted and put off his stride by the strength of the wind and waves. This is what the Devil does: he points to the wind and the waves. He tries to push our attention to the bread that is missing or the stones that are present. He tries to convince us that our status as God's children and our worth as human beings is connected to the tangible things that we can see.

Like the people demanding for a sign, we begin to be doers who walk only by sight, but as Jesus points out in his reply to the Devil, that is not what following God is about. Paul puts it this way: 'The man who finds life, will find it through trusting God' (Galatians 3:11).

And in Jesus's response, he makes it clear that we do not live by bread alone but by God's Word. Life is not found in tangible things; life is found through trusting God. Hebrews 11 says that whoever wants to please God must believe that God exists, and not that there is 'a God', but that there is 'this God'—that the God revealed through Jesus and his Word is real.

This is the place to which Jesus is trying to get the people who gather around him. You do not need manna to fall from the sky before you believe; trust in who God is.

In Matthew 6:25–33, Jesus reassures us with these words:

> Therefore I tell you, do not worry about your life, what you will eat or drink; or about your body, what you will wear. Is not life more than food, and the body more than clothes? Look at the birds of the air; they do not sow or reap or store away in barns,

and yet your heavenly Father feeds them. Are you not much more valuable than they? Can any one of you by worrying add a single hour to your life?

And why do you worry about clothes? See how the flowers of the field grow. They do not labour or spin. Yet I tell you that not even Solomon in all his splendour was dressed like one of these. If that is how God clothes the grass of the field, which is here today and tomorrow is thrown into the fire, will he not much more clothe you—you of little faith? So do not worry, saying, 'What shall we eat?' or 'What shall we drink?' or 'What shall we wear?' For the pagans run after all these things, and your heavenly Father knows that you need them. But seek first his kingdom and his righteousness, and all these things will be given to you as well.

The bottom line is that God knows how to look after his own. He knows where our hunger is, he knows what we thirst for, and he knows where we are vulnerable. He is not in the dark, and he is not indifferent; he is working things out. Where we feel vulnerable and exposed, he will clothe us, wrapping us with robes of righteousness and unfailing love. And where we are hungry, he will satisfy our every need.

My dad loved to quote Robert Sculler during times of perceived inactivity from God: 'God's delay is not God's denial.'

Whatever may be before us, be it stone or bread, does not change who God is and his commitment to us. It does not change the truth or authenticity of his Word. And this is where our faith lies, not in the tangible things the enemy suggests, but in the never-ending grace and the unchanging nature of our God. Holding on to these truths, even in the presence of stones, will help us see beyond the stones. Because if God is good and is with us, then we know that we will be fine. As someone once said, when you feel down, look up.

There may be no bread at particular points in our journey, but there is always God. We always have his Word with us, and like Jesus, when we make his Word our truth, we overcome the Devil's lies. Sometimes the bread we think we need is not actually what we require. If Jesus had, for instance, given in to the people's demand for a miracle, it would have created a people whose appetites were whetted but whose hearts remained unchanged. The Devil loves to whet our appetites while destroying our hearts. Jesus's plan is to transform our hearts while feeding us in such a way that we hunger no more.

Jesus dismisses the Devil's ploy, but the Devil doesn't give up.

His next trick is to offer us the opportunity to be at the centre of the story, to go from being just another character in God's story to being the key player in our own. It is what he offers up to Jesus when he asks him to jump down from the temple, to go for the spectacular and aim for the jugular. It is an old trick he usually goes back to. After all, it worked with Eve.

Eve was blown away by the idea of being her own God, the idea of leading rather than following, the idea of being served rather than serving—the lure of pride and glory.

It's the lure that knocks out even the best of us.

The temptation to shine for ourselves is always with us. Everyone likes to receive praise, and everyone likes for their achievements and abilities to be celebrated. The enemy offers that alternative path, a path where we pursue our own agenda, our own dreams.

In life, we are handed two scripts. In one, we are the main character in a story about ourselves, and in the other, we are part of a supporting cast in the story God is telling. In one the soundtrack is Frank Sinatra's 'I did it my way,' and in the other it's a soundtrack of surrender: 'I did it God's way.'

———

Which script are we acting out?

The Devil offered Jesus a path to glory, offers to make it about him, but his offer was declined. Jesus understood that this journey was about what God was doing, and he didn't want it any other way. He had complete faith in the plan of his Father, that the path God had called him to was one filled with life, and that we shine brightest when we are following God's will for our lives.

Every writer is taught that there are three important elements of a good script. The first is to have a brilliant lead character, someone whom the whole story revolves around. Everything is seen from the point of view of the lead character, and the whole story revolves around how this person gets from A to B. Every other character is there to support the main character and aid in his or her cause.

Like the people in the parable of the feast, one of the reasons we decline the invitation to sit at the table with Jesus is that we are still at the centre of our story. We are still acting out a script where we are the main character, and everything is about us getting what we want, about our happy endings.

It is *my* dreams, *my* job, and *my* relationships, and we are not willing to hand them over to God. We are happy for Jesus to join us for the ride, but we expect him to toe the line, or at least to understand that these things are too important, so he needs to let them be. He should agree to the path we've chosen rather than suggest an alternative. We are happy for him to sit in the car as long as we're the ones who are driving. He is simply a supporting act to our story.

Another important element of a good script is intention and obstacle. There is something the lead character wants, and there is something making it difficult to get it. If we are the lead character in the script we are living out, this will be all wrong for us as well. Our lives will be all about what we want and the things stopping us from getting it. We will end up being selfish, inward-looking people who have no care for anything or anyone but ourselves. Jesus is not interested in getting glory for himself, so he declines the offer to jump from the temple. His path is for God's glory.

Also, a life lived where we are the central character is not as beautiful as it sounds. Adam and Eve swapped the Garden of Eden for an alternative path, one where they led rather than followed, and it didn't end well. We are still suffering the effects of that decision today. Because having our eyes focused on personal glory ultimately creates a miserable life and a miserable world to boot. When our lives are driven by our own intentions and obstacles, we are easily discouraged by how big the obstacles are and how far away the prize is from us. It leads to anxiety, worry, and ultimately darkness. We who are the light of the world become part of the darkness, and we who are the salt become part of the bitterness.

But a life focused on God's intention and obstacle is one that seeks after the kingdom of God diligently. And the person living such a life knows that our success in our journey here on earth is not dependent on what we are capable of doing but on what God is capable of. So it doesn't matter if no one says we're awesome, as long as through our lives they see God is awesome. And it doesn't matter if no one worships us, as long as we play a part in getting many to worship God. This is Jesus's vision, and so even after some of his most impressive miracles, his instruction is for those he's blessed to keep it quiet. He doesn't need glory; he just needs us to know that God is real and that he loves us.

And finally, we are told as writers that we have to show, not tell. It's not enough to tell people who a character is; we need to show it with the events of the character's life. When we are the lead character, we want to show everyone who we are. Our every thought and action is intended to draw attention to ourselves. The Devil's plan is to get us to operate this way, and that was his temptation to Jesus.

But Jesus lives a life that points others to God, and this is the life of a disciple. I don't know about you, but I don't want to be my own god. I don't want my life and the lives of others to depend on what I can or cannot do. I am limited, weak, and flawed; besides, I know someone who is excellent at being God. I'd rather live to point the attention and focus towards him.

A path where it's all about us also tends to be a very lonely one. Every setback is a mountain, and every disappointment is an insurmountable challenge. On this path, everyone is a threat. We are untrusting and unflinching, and it eats at us until there is nothing left.

The truth is, the things being sold at the wide gates, this offer to be God, it never truly satisfies. It's an unbelievable sham. Adam and Eve found this out in time, and we will too. That path never delivers on what it promises, and it doesn't have the capacity to give us what we're searching for.

What we need lies on the narrow path, where Jesus is. The other path only leads to frustration. The job, the relationship, the possessions, and all the things we pursue on the path of self—in the end, we find that they fall short. They don't bring peace or rest. They are at best temporary in their ability to affirm us, and they don't last forever. As seasons come and go, as the world moves and changes, so do these things and their ability to satisfy us or bring us affirmation.

The path of discipleship is one of humility and surrender, one where we are able to give God his place as the central character, a place where we are willing to stop everything to follow him, even if it means changing course. It is bringing our relationships, businesses, dreams, and possessions to the feast and making them available to the Master.

Yes, Jesus could have jumped from the temple in a *Mission: Impossible* type of way. Yes, he could have delivered some amazing sign for the people. Both might have gotten him worship and reverence, and maybe even a greater following (it would definitely have gotten him better feedback to his sermon). But it would not have led to life for those involved, and Jesus's main concern was to deliver light and life to those around him. The same is true for us. A path that is all about us may bring us fame and platitudes, but it won't bring us life or purpose. Only God's path has the ability to do that.

So again the Devil was dismissed, but he still had one last card to play, and it was the most audacious offer of all. He flat-out offered Jesus a completely different story, a brand-new way of doing things, a new take on life. The Devil dared to suggest that Jesus worship him.

And his selling point was this: if Jesus were to agree to do things his way, he could have the whole world, and he would have it without needing to go to the cross. Satan would give him a different kingdom.

'You want these people? I'll give you these people. All you have to do is bow down to me.'

Sound familiar?

Have you ever felt the enemy offering you a different kingdom to chase after? A kingdom of money, sex, and rock and roll? No talk about discipleship, no talk about surrender or living by faith and so forth, just good ol' fun and games all the way? Do what you like and pursue what you want. Sounds fun, right?

The Devil is a very good salesman, I'll give him that. He is very good at selling doo-doo like it is expensive jewellery. From the moment he got Eve to give up the kingdom God had set ahead of her in exchange for a shot at creating her own, he hasn't quit. He's always pitching that sale to us, the idea that there is a different way to do things and it is infinitely more fun. Why stick to God's plan when there is an easier one available?

What the Devil doesn't reveal, of course, are the words written in the fine print, the words that reveal the true offer. These are the words explaining that he isn't offering us a chance to build our own kingdom or to be our own God. What he is offering is a swap deal, where we swap a heavenly kingdom of righteousness, peace, and joy in the Holy Spirit for a dark, joyless, and empty one with him, and where we swap a merciful and loving God for a vicious and cruel one.

It's like those commercials where the salesperson talks so effusively about the product, saying that it cures all ills, brings world peace, and is the solution to every problem. But then, just at the end, they rush through the disclaimer, which pretty much says, 'This product doesn't do any of the things we just said it did.'

The Devil is the same. He screams out, 'Do it my way, and you will get all your heart desires.' In truth, all that lies in his offer is death.

It happened to Judas. He swapped the life of a disciple for the pursuit of wealth. He thought that the riches would make him happier than God did. The same was true of David when he went after Bathsheba. He thought having her would make him feel more alive than God could. Both men realised how wrong they were.

They should have read the fine print.

Judas was unable to live with himself and committed suicide, and David's life spiralled out of control, culminating in the death of his son.

It's easy to judge these men, and many do, but the truth is that we have all walked in their shoes. Like Esau, we, at one point or the other, have traded out birthright for a bowl of soup. The hunger we had in that moment, in that phase of our lives, felt more important than who we were as disciples of Jesus, and so we traded in.

God's heartbroken cry to David is one we may have heard repeated to us in different ways. In the book of 2 Samuel, chapter 12, following David's fall,

God reminds David of their journey together and how he has been with him and sustained him through it, and then he says these words in verse 8: 'And if all this had been too little, I would have given you even more.'

The Devil tries to paint a picture of a God who doesn't care for us, one who just wants control. He tells us that it is he, the Devil, who offers us freedom in the guise of a different kind of kingdom. He implores us to experience freedom by feeding that desire that we have and encouraging us to go for whatever we want without thinking too much about it. He says to Eve in Genesis 3, 'Did God really say, "You must not eat from any tree in the garden"? … You will not certainly die, God knows that when you eat from it your eyes will be opened, and you will be like God, knowing good and evil.'

He creates this idea that God sends us on difficult paths and that his plans are hard and tedious, aimed at reining us in. He convinces us that a life spent following Jesus is a joyless one.

I always remember from my younger days that when I would buy into this lie and go off on a different road, living a different way and pursuing a different kingdom, it wasn't long before, like the Prodigal Son, I would find myself sitting in a pen of pigs and thinking to myself, *Life chasing after God's kingdom was a lot better than this.*

They say you never know what you have till it's gone, and sometimes we take the peace, rest, and joy we have in God's love for granted. It's only when we're sitting in front of a bunch of bulky pigs, begging them for a spoon of dirt, that we realise just how good we had it in our Father's house.

God is always looking out for us, as he was for David. And if we will trust him and choose to seek his kingdom, prioritising that search above all others, we will discover just how worthwhile the journey is.

In God's plan, the one that is about the pursuit of his kingdom, lies a future worth hoping for, just as he revealed through Jeremiah: 'I know what I'm doing. I have it all planned out—plans to take care of you, not abandon you, plans to give you the future you hope for' (Jeremiah 29:11).

In the enemy's story, the one that is about going after other kingdoms, lies a future filled with nightmares.

Peter understood this. He had walked with Jesus and had come to believe that a tomorrow that was worth having was one that had Jesus in it, not in the passenger seat, but leading the way. So when Jesus asked the Twelve whether they too wanted to forsake him, he answered, 'Lord, to whom shall we go? You have the words of eternal life. And we have come to believe and to know that you are the Holy One of God.'

Peter put his faith in who Jesus is. For him there were no alternatives. Only Jesus held the key to life and completeness. He wasn't wrong.

5

Smelly Feet and Dirty Hands

(John 13:1–17)

Imagine the CEO of a multibillion-pound enterprise approaching the desk of one of his employees, a big bunch of kitchen paper in hand. The employee has just spilled coffee all over his own table, and without being asked, the CEO goes to the kitchen, gets some wipes, and as though it were a completely normal thing to do, begins to wipe the table clean. That would be quite something to behold, wouldn't it?

Jesus stunned his disciples similarly when he approached them, basin in hand, and proceeded to wash and dry their feet. This was no 'luxury' task or PR stunt; Jesus was getting his hands well and truly dirty, performing not just one of the most mundane tasks but also one of the most undesirable ones. It would be interesting to know what the disciples were thinking when their Master picked up each of their smelly feet and gave them a good shine.

Peter, as always, didn't disappoint.

For him it was a bit too much, and while the other disciples were content to keep their thoughts to themselves and just watch on in wonder, he spoke out in protest.

'Lord, are you going to wash my feet?' he exclaimed.

It just didn't make sense to Peter. Why would his Lord, someone he believed to be the Son of God, wash his feet? He couldn't allow it.

I can see where Peter was coming from.

Even at the best of times, our feet are not something we throw about in people's faces. You wouldn't want anyone going anywhere near them at the end of a long tenuous day. You wouldn't let your enemy near them, let alone someone you loved or respected. But even as Peter protested, Jesus said to him, 'Unless I wash you, you have no part with me.'

Just like our dirty feet, we all have a side of us that we don't like others to see, a side of us that we think is too dark and ugly to be lovable.

When we do relationships, we compartmentalise in a way almost similar to the temple Solomon built for God in the Old Testament. That temple had different components or courts, and who could enter which court was dependent on one's status. Depending on whether you were Jew or Gentile, male or female, high priest or common lad, you were either allowed or excluded from access to particular parts of the temple. The chief priest got to access the Holy of Holies, the place where the fullness of God was revealed, everyone else had to settle for tit bits.

We do the same with our own temples.

We've got an outer court, if you like, which is a part of us we make accessible to the general public. Our Facebook and Instagram profiles if you like, where we portray the doctored version of who we really are. Anyone can see this version of us. It is safe and doesn't reveal much.

Then there are the inner courts, and here we allow ourselves to be a little more vulnerable. This is the side we show to our family and close friends, those who are more likely to love us despite our little hang-ups. Here, to some extent, we allow the pictures we portray to be less doctored, a little more of the original us is visible. Those we let in here are better able to describe us. They know our likes and dislikes. They even know a little bit of our flaws and fears.

And then there is the holy of holies. In this segment of our lives, all the make-up is off; there is no doctoring. All that's left is us—warts and all. This is our 'dirty feet' room, and hardly anyone gets the privilege of entering in. And with good reason.

It is not a very attractive place and is therefore something we want to keep hidden. Some people go through life never letting anyone into this place. And while for the temple the holy of holies was a place of extreme purity, for us this room is anything but that. There is a big sign on the door that reads, *'Keep out!'*

Where do we place Jesus in our interaction with him?

Firstly it's worth mentioning that Jesus does not compartmentalise when it comes to us. He doesn't deny us access to his love and presence based on our 'status'. There is no outer or inner courts with Jesus, all are welcome to know and access Jesus fully and completely. Perhaps we don't because it is us who are scared or reluctant to allow him access to the real us; to every inner chamber of our lives.

Jesus desires to dwell in every room in our hearts, he wants access to the real us; to our holy of holies where the full extent of who we are is revealed. Only when we let him in here can he truly change us and bring about real transformation in our lives. But there is a darkness that we feel is a step too far, even for Jesus. We can't let him in there, because letting him in there would mean we would have to admit that this room exists, and it's not something we want to do. We've sprayed air fresheners across the room to stop ourselves and others from smelling the stench. We've hidden it beautifully all this time. But then Jesus shows up. Basin in hand, a towel across his waist, asking us to let him have our feet.

We struggle to do this because we don't even love this version of us, so how can anyone else? We expect rejection, for Jesus to meet those stinky feet with an expression of disappointment and disgust.

But God is not afraid of our darkness. It does not put him off.

Let me let you in on a secret. When Jesus chose you and me to be his disciples, he knew all about the dirty feet. He knew about the side of us we never let anyone see. He knew us at our absolute worst, and that was when he came to us and said, 'Follow me.' He did that for Peter at the beginning, and he does the same for us.

The Bible tells us that God shows his great love for us in that while we were sinners, Christ died for us. God did not give us his best when we were at our best; he did so when we were at our worst. And that does not change. God is constantly giving us his best, wherever we are. Whether we are shining as light or are consumed by darkness, whether we are thriving or faltering, God is always giving us his best. Why? Well, because he loves us and because that is who he is. In his second letter to Timothy, Paul shares this aspect of God's character: 'If we are unfaithful, he remains faithful, for he cannot deny who he is' (2 Timothy 2:13).

But the time comes in our journey when God wants to deal with the darkness. Because how can we love others when we don't love ourselves? And how can we be light when we are holding on to darkness, or salt when we are drowning in bitterness? At some point, that darkness will hinder us, and the smelly feet will prevent us from running, unless we hand them over to Jesus and let him wash them.

It's not easy to come face-to-face with that side of us, let alone let the most righteous of all see it. But hiding only makes matters worse. David's story tells us as much. The more he tried to cover his tracks, the worse things got. The darkness grew and grew until, by the end of the story, he had not just slept with the wife of one of his most loyal men, but he had also arranged his death. He later coined these words in Psalm 35: 'Blessed is the one whose transgressions are forgiven, whose sins are covered. Blessed is the one whose sin the Lord does not count against them and in whose spirit is no deceit. When I kept silent, my bones wasted away through my groaning all day long ... Then I acknowledged my sin to you and did not cover up my iniquity ... And you forgave the guilt of my sin.'

Too often we choose to be silent, opting for plausible deniability as David did. We do the ostrich thing and bury our heads in the sand, hoping that if we don't confront the problem, it will just go away on its own. We find nice shoes to stick our smelly feet into and hope that in this way they hurt no one. If we can't see them, and if no one else can, then we should be fine, right?

The problem though with shoes is that no matter how nice they look, eventually they have to come off.

Jesus comes to us as the light that shines in the darkness, as the light that the darkness cannot overcome. Whether it is fear or worry, lusts or addiction, bitterness or hurts—whatever the darkness is, wherever it lies, whoever caused it, Jesus is the light that overcomes it all. He turned David's darkness into light (Psalm 18:28), and he wants to do the same for you and me. We don't need to stumble around with the lights off. We don't need to be eaten up by guilt or carry the stench of sin. Jesus is a Saviour who gets his hands dirty, his beautiful nail-pierced hands, hands that were bloodied to keep our feet clean.

And just as Jesus said to Peter, that if he does not let him wash his feet, Peter cannot be part of his journey, we cannot be part of Jesus's journey if we do not let him see our stinky feet. Jesus is not after superficial relationships. He doesn't just want to be our Facebook friend or someone who randomly likes our best Instagram pictures. He wants to go with us to where the waters are deep and the roads are hard. He wants to walk with us through the good and the bad, at our best and our worst. He wants to help us, if we'll allow ourselves to be helped.

After Jesus washes the disciples' feet, he urges them to follow his example and wash each other's feet. Throughout his ministry Jesus surrounds himself with people at their most broken state, and through his love and acceptance they find the grace to be made whole. He does the same for us, choosing us while we are broken, when our feet are at their dirtiest point and washing them clean.

A church gathering can sometimes be a place where only your best self is welcome. We'll take your pretty face and your nicely toned muscles. We'll take those lovely hats and shoes all day long, but please, please, do not come into our building with your feet stinking. Find a way to hide them. We may not use those words, but we definitely pass that message across to each other. It's funny, because on one side, we appreciate that Jesus is not afraid or put off by the parts of us that are ugly, but then when we notice such ugliness in someone else, we keep them at a 'safe' distance. We run away from smelly feet and do not want to get our hands dirty, even though someone perfect got his hands dirty for us.

We celebrate the success stories, the answered prayers, and the baptism testimonies, but that is all we are sometimes willing to recognise or accept. We'll welcome the recovering alcoholic but not the struggling alcoholic.

We'll welcome the former drug addict but not the struggling porn addict. We pick and choose where we show grace. And in the end we never get the basin out, let alone do any washing.

But Jesus is clear in his instruction to us: washing feet is part of what we're about. We are to have the humility to love and serve each other irrespective of where others are in their journey. We are to show grace irrespective of the dirt on display, because that is what Jesus did for us. We cannot change people, but we can love them, and that's what we're called to do. Jesus lays out this vision to us. He calls us to represent perfect love and grace, to love the unlovable and forgive the unforgivable, to reach out to the marginalised and speak up for the oppressed, to get our hands dirty. Darkness should not scare us; it should inspire us, be it darkness in our world or in the life of others. We are, after all, called to be the light of the world, just like Jesus. And what did John say about that light? That darkness cannot overcome it. It can try, but in the end, the light of God within us will always win, will always shine through.

I think it is important at this point to reflect on an important element of the story. Look at John 13:3–4 again: 'Jesus knew that the Father had put all things under his power, and that he had come from God and was returning to God; *so he got up* from the meal, took off his outer clothing, and wrapped a towel around his waist.'

Verse 4 in particular tells us that Jesus, *knowing who he was and what he was called to do*, 'got up'. That knowledge inspired him to step up and do what he did. It didn't make him proud, or selfish, or entitled. The passage doesn't say, Jesus knew that the Father had put all things under his power, and that he had come from God and was returning to God, so he ordered the disciples to wash his feet. There were twelve of them after all, so there were enough toes to go round.

Empowered and at peace with who he was, Jesus had no problem giving his life for others.

This world calls us to look out for number one, to aspire to a greatness that is shown through our ability to dominate others. The world calls us to dominate in relationships, to dominate in our careers, and to dominate in life. The world's vision is to make it about ourselves.

Jesus called us to a different way: strength shown through humility, self-awareness displayed through looking out for others. Whatever gifts or abilities we are blessed with, they were not given to produce big-headedness. They were given so we get up, so that we step up to the plate of giving life and washing feet. We are blessed to bless, loved to love, and forgiven to forgive.

As we learn more about who we are, that we came from God and will return to him, and that all we have he gave to us, the hope is that we too will get up from where we're sitting, that we too will wrap a towel round our waist and pick up a basin of water, that we will charge purposefully into a darkened world with our light shining bright and get our hands dirty.

Something tells me there's a lot of needy feet out there.

6

The F-word

(Matthew 18:21–35)

Forgiveness is one of those things that I struggle with. I always have. I remember as a little boy going up to my mum and asking her, 'Do I still have to forgive someone even if they haven't asked to be forgiven?' I was always looking for a loophole, a get-out clause. Perhaps Peter was looking for the same when he approached Jesus with his question in the passage in Matthew: 'How many times should I forgive my brother?'

He even suggested an answer: perhaps seven times? Surely that was reasonable enough. I hear you, Peter.

Jesus's response was to say not seven times, but seventy times seven. In other words, we should forgive those who wrong us every time they need forgiveness. How many times should I forgive someone who hurt me? Every single time. Whoa, slow down, Jesus.

There are two ways to look at this. Either we can look at it as a burden, or we can look at it as the amazing blessing that it is. Because when Jesus asks us to give our forgiveness every time it is needed, what that tells us is that he does the same for us.

How often does God forgive us? Every time we need it.

No matter how often or where we've screwed up, whenever we need his forgiveness, God will give it to us. Jesus goes on to underline this point in the parable that follows. Notice that in the story, the master doesn't just give the servant more time to pay back his debt. He doesn't just show patience or set up a direct debit. He doesn't just reduce the debt; he cancels it in its entirety. As far as he is concerned, those debts were never owed. This is what God does for us.

David put it this way in Psalm 103:12: 'As far as the east is from the west, so far has he removed our transgressions from us.'

In other words, God does not associate those sins with us. He doesn't see us as the person who lied or drank too much. He doesn't refer to us as the promiscuous or unfaithful one. Whatever the sin may have been, as far as he is concerned it has nothing to do with us. He separates it from us, as far as the east is from the west, and he views us without the prejudice of our sins.

All he asks in return is that we do the same for others.

Paul put it this way in his letter to the Ephesian church: 'Forgive each other just as in Christ, God forgave you' (Ephesians 4:32).

If God chooses to forgive us, even though he is perfect and would be fully justified not to, and if he is merciful to us, even though, like the master in the story, he has the power to punish not just us but everyone who carries our name, then we should show forgiveness and mercy to those who wrong us, shouldn't we?

God calls us not just to forgive, but to forgive as he forgave us in Christ. That means to completely remove the prejudice, to no longer look at those people who wronged us through the lens of what they did wrong. Be it the difficult parent, the unfaithful friend, or the horrible boss, forgiving the godly way means we remove the negative adjectives. We no longer see the offender for what they did wrong.

As far as the east is from the west, we remove their sins from them.

Does that sound difficult? It sure does to Judge Grudge over here. It's a good thing we don't have to do it on our own power. We can rely on the strength of Christ. Paul says that we can do all things through Christ who gives us strength, and I believe forgiveness falls into the category of 'all things'. If you, like me, struggle with this, or if you have been badly hurt, you're definitely going to need a strength bigger than your own to carry this commandment out. The good news is that such strength is readily available; all we need to do is ask for it.

As someone once said, forgiveness is a decision we make every day. We can choose to forgive or to remain resentful. I don't know what it is about staying resentful, but it seems somehow to be more desirable to us. Well, it does to me anyway. The feeling of resentment and the release of forgiveness are two very different emotions. When we choose to let go of the hurt and forgive, it actually feels good. A burden is lifted, and joy is possible again. Still, for some reason, we feel an urge to hold on to the pain. And we can hold onto it for so long, it begins to define us. And it defines us in ways that are in complete contrast to what Jesus has to offer.

We cannot be people who are defined by grace and bitterness at the same time; it just doesn't work. We can't take our identity from the grace of God and from our hurts. One will have to give way to the other, and it is our choice which that is.

In the end we need to ask ourselves, *Is any hurt more valuable to hold on to than the grace of God?*

And that is the problem with an unforgiving life, it is all-consuming, so much so that we struggle to experience God's grace and mercy for ourselves. In the parable we read earlier, the servant is handed over to jailers who torture him until he pays back all he owes. This is what resentment does: it tortures us. The anger and the pain consumes us until it becomes us. This is because we can't escape the reality that we ultimately morph into the things that monopolize our focus. Perhaps this is why forgiveness is a big deal for Jesus. He touches on this topic consistently, always urging us to live lives personified by grace.

Because the trap of an unforgiving life is this: not only does it define us in ways that are in conflict with who we are in Jesus, but it also separates us from God's grace. A heart that doesn't forgive struggles to have faith in God's forgiveness, and a person who is impatient with the flaws in others struggles to recognise God's patience with his or her own flaws.

In Matthew 6:15, Jesus is quite direct when he says, 'If you do not forgive others their sins, your Father will not forgive your sins.'

It makes you wonder: Is God's forgiveness dependent on our capacity to forgive others? Is his grace conditional?

I don't think that's necessarily the case. God is I Am after all. He is who he is. Nothing and no one can make him change or bend to their will. There is no adjective that can put him in a box. *He is.* What I do believe is that our capacity to experience God's forgiveness is limited by our inability to forgive. If we are very unforgiving people, guilt will always eat us up, and we will continually carry a burden we don't need to. Believing in God's grace will always be difficult for those who live ungracious lives.

But choosing to forgive someone is not always an easy decision to make. There's a reason we feel hurt in the first place, and most times it is not unreasonable. Sometimes there are hurts that are too unspeakable and pains that go more than skin-deep. Is God insensitive to these? Does it not matter to him that we are in pain and who caused it?

Thankfully, God is neither insensitive to our hurt nor unconcerned about our pain. David says about him in Psalm 56:8, 'You keep track of all my sorrows. You have collected all my tears in your bottle. You have recorded each one in your book.'

Does God care that we've been hurt? You bet he does, so much so that he doesn't forget. In fact he keeps a record of how often we have been hurt, and he keeps an eye on all our sorrows. What he wants is for us to trust him with the pain, to trust him to take care of us and to be released from the weight of the burden that it brings. Jesus's teaching in Matthew 6:25–34 can be summarised as such: focus your attention on bringing life to others because God's attention is focused on bringing life to you. And he never takes his eye off the boil.

I remember coming to God years ago about an individual who had wronged me. I felt very bitter about what had happened, and I needed God to do something about it. That's when I heard God say to me, 'ND, I love you, but I love that person too.'

Suffice to say I wasn't happy with this response. I felt betrayed and completely let down. How can the one I know to turn to in a time like this be declaring love for the very person who's done me harm? I was not impressed. But in the midst of my unhappiness, God spoke words to me that I have never forgotten: 'He prepares a table before me, in the presence of my enemies' (Psalm 23:6).

I had read that psalm so many times before, but on that day I heard it in a new way. That day he said, 'I will bless and take care of you in such a way that the hurts won't matter anymore.'

And those words have never failed. They proved true in that particular grief I was dealing with, and they have proved true ever since. He always takes care of me right where it hurts. The moment I let go, I see his grace surround me to the point where I don't feel the pain anymore; the blessings he has given me are greater than the wrongs that were done.

This is not a promise specific to me or to David; it is one that God makes to all his children. We don't need to hold on to the pain, because God already has it and is doing something about it. If we'll let him take care of us, he will heal us and fill our lives with the beauty of his presence. But we have to let go.

We have to choose to focus on the goodness of God rather than on the evil of the world.

Many times in my journey with God, I have found that he does not forget my pain or my tears. At the time of being hurt, I may have felt it was a burden I needed to carry alone, that I had to find a way to put the offender in his or her place. But whenever I've made the choice to trust in God's grace instead, to focus on it rather than on the wrongs, it has always been the better choice. At the time it may have felt like choosing the narrow path over one that seemed more accessible, but that is the path that has always brought life.

The blessing of God's grace is so immense that nothing is worth giving it up for. And so the F-word, *forgiveness*, doesn't have to be one we dread. It doesn't have to feel unfair or burdensome. There is life in forgiveness. It is a better path and a better way to live, one that lands us in God's care. And he prepares a pretty good table.

How often should you forgive? As often as you are forgiven, and that is every single time.

7

Dealing with Chaff

(Luke 22:31–34)

Chaff defn : worthless things; rubbish

Wouldn't it be great if after we made the decision to follow Jesus and become his disciples, the Devil just left us alone?

Wouldn't it be amazing if he accepted defeat graciously and moved on, leaving us to continue growing at our own pace? I mean, wouldn't that just be fantastic? And after we place our trust in Jesus as Lord and Saviour, after we embrace our identity as God's children, wouldn't it be wonderful if we stopped struggling with negative emotions and desiring things we shouldn't?

We long to be the selfless, joy-giving, grace-exuding folk who live worry-free, abundant lives every day, but often that is not our reality. Sometimes it's not even close to our reality. We aim for the righteous life in Christ we are called to. We aspire to that, but life keeps snapping at our heels, and that old self keeps popping up. Our old self, that lifelong nemesis of ours that we thought we'd put to the sword, but the stubborn thing keeps trying to perform a resurrection. And every now and then, as life snaps at our heels, the chaff within comes to the fore.

Ah, chaff! The worthless stuff that we supposedly left behind in order to follow Jesus. Why is it still present? Paul expressed the same exasperation we feel in Romans 7:18–19: 'I have the desire to do what is good, but I cannot carry it out. For I do not do the good I want to do, but the evil I do not want to do—this I keep doing.'

Ever feel like that? If we're completely honest, there are times when we feel like Al Pacino's character in *The Godfather*: 'Just when we think we're out, it drags us back in.' Oh, what to do about chaff?

You may be sitting there thinking, *I haven't got any chaff. I'm perfect me.*

This is the exact same way Peter felt when Jesus suggested that his faith was about to be tested.

'Lord, I am ready to go with you to prison and to death,' he said.

He was sure there was no chaff within him, just a heart that purred for Jesus.

We've all been there. I definitely have. When I was around eighteen or nineteen years old, my relationship with God experienced a big growth spurt. My prayer life was going places, as was my understanding of God's Word. I felt on fire spiritually. I felt unstoppable. Like Moses, I felt like God met me in my room and we had good conversations together. I was buzzing, and I then I got a bit cocky. To be honest, I got a great deal cocky and then some.

One evening as I was spending time alone with God, I stopped bang in the middle of my prayers and declared foolishly, 'Lord, I don't think I could ever sin again. I just don't think it's possible. I know too much!'

I'm not sure who or what possessed me to utter such rubbish. I'll blame it on youthful exuberance, but the bottom line is that I said it, and I was convinced of it. Like Peter, I was sure of myself. 'Lord, I will follow you even if it kills me!'

It turned out that this was not the only similarity I have with Peter. Shortly after my bold declarations, the Devil showed up with his sifter, and, boy, did he find a lot of chaff floating around. The following year I crashed so badly, I should have been written off as damaged beyond repair. I went from riding high on a spiritual wave to paddling in the mud. The decline was remarkable.

And this is what the Devil does. He pokes around in our lives looking for chaff, and he doesn't play fair. His strategy is to identify where we are most vulnerable and attack it. I imagine his motto is something like 'Where there's vulnerability, there's chaff.'

And so he shows up with his sifter, having sussed out a possible chink in the armour or sniffed a considerable whiff of vulnerability. The worst thing is, most times he's right. More often than not, where there's vulnerability, there usually is chaff.

Jesus finds us full of chaff when we come to him. We are full of lots of things that did not belong in us: misplaced ideas, perspectives, desires, dreams, habits; the list is never ending. When we came to Jesus, we were broken and in dire need of saving. And Jesus accepted us and took us in. He didn't ask us to go sort ourselves out and then come back and follow him. Just as he did with Peter, he embraced us with all our brokenness and gave us an invitation to do life at his side, with an unwavering faith that the more we do life with him, the more we will be transformed, until we are completely chaff-free.

As Paul talks about his battle with chaff in Romans 7, he makes this concluding statement: 'Who will rescue me from this body that is subject to death? Thanks be to God, who delivers me through Jesus Christ our Lord!'

While the Devil is the ultimate chaff spotter, Jesus is our supreme chaff remover, and Jesus never fails.

But to experience the chaff-removing work of Jesus in our lives, we need to commit to walking with God in humility on a day-to-day basis. Paul in Romans 12:3 talks about not thinking of ourselves more highly than we should. The prophet Micah put it this way: 'He has shown you, O mortal, what is good. And what does the Lord require of you? To act justly and to love mercy and to walk humbly with your God' (Micah 6:8).

This is because the Devil has two methods through which he tries to make chaff stick. One is through pride, and the other is through isolation.

Pride puts us in a place where God cannot reach us. A prideful life is not characterised by a heart that surrenders, ears that listen, or eyes that see. It is why God despises pride so much. He knows that pride leaves us vulnerable to the enemy. Both Peter and I found that to be painfully true.

Up till this point, Peter was a big-headed disciple who believed he could take on anything and anyone. He learnt in the end, like I did, that we are completely reliant on the grace that God gives, that we can do all things not by our own will or intelligence, but through Christ who gives us strength.

The enemy also attempts to isolate us from Jesus. He knows that Jesus is our source of strength and that once we are cut off from the vine that is Jesus, we can do nothing. The Devil manages to isolate Peter from Jesus on that fateful night, and with his eyes off his Lord, Peter crumbles.

When we are removed from the presence of God, chaff reigns supreme.

The key to overcoming is walking with God day-to-day and in complete humility.

Paul talks about being drunk with the Holy Spirit rather than with wine (Ephesians 5:18), and what he is saying is that we should allow the Holy Spirit to have the same influence over our lives as wine has over alcoholics. Our every mood and behaviour, the way we spend our time and money, and our whole perspective on life should be driven by the Holy Spirit.

This is a chaff-free life.

The Devil understands this, and his plan is to usher us into a 'Spirit Prohibition' era. But we must press on with a thirst for the Holy Spirit, a desire to get completely drunk on the grace and power of God.

Following the same alcohol analogy from Paul, let's consider what it takes to be drunk with wine. First we'd need to go somewhere where there is wine: to a bar, a supermarket, or a fridge. Just sitting in a room thinking of drinking wine won't get anyone drunk. Next we'd need to invest in it, either buying it from the shop or bar, or maybe just opening the fridge and getting it out. Because just staring at the alcohol is not going to do the job. There is a scene in the American comedy *Friends* where Joey Tribbiani suggests selling a product by replacing the line 'Pick up a bag today' with 'Point at a bag today.' Pointing isn't going to do it; we need to pick it up. And then finally, we'd need to drink the wine, and keep drinking it at that. You don't get drunk on one bottle; you need to keep going.

The same is true if we are to live chaff-free lives.

First, we need to put ourselves in a place where God can reach us. This is a fundamental first step. Paul talks about not getting in the way of what the Holy Spirit is doing. Instead we should position ourselves where he can work through us. We need to go where the Holy Spirit is.

We do this by making concerted efforts to walk with God daily. Get a good Bible and devotional, be part of a local church, join a life group of other disciples, and create space for prayer. If you're musically inclined, buy music that brings you into God's presence; if you're a reader, buy books that do the same. Whatever and wherever it is, find a way to be where the Spirit of God can reach you, physically, mentally, and in your heart.

And then once you are positioned, you have to follow through on it. Unlike Joey, don't just point. Pick it up. Don't just sit in the pews of the local church; be part of it. Once you join a life group, commit to going. Commit to using your experiences to bless others and learning from theirs. Walk with God through his Word, and walk with him in prayer. Play the music and read the books.

And once you start on this road, you must stick to it. Just like you don't get drunk on the first glass of wine, you don't get filled with the Holy Spirit without persevering. Jesus, in the parable of the sower, spoke about the seed that falls on good soil, which is representative of those who hear the Word, retain it, and persevere with it.

The key to avoid the Devil trapping us in a chaff-controlled prison is to maintain humble hearts and stay close to God. But should we fall, should we find ourselves choking on chaff for whatever reason, the good news is that God's grace is more than sufficient. Our story with Jesus doesn't end with our mistakes. Peter's life is evidence of this.

Peter was about to be tested, and despite his protestations, he would fail miserably. He would have three goes at getting it right, but each time he would tank even worse than the previous opportunity. Jesus knew this was coming, and his response was to pray for Peter. He did not freeze him out, and he didn't abandon him or express disappointment; he prayed for Peter that his faith would not fail.

He prays for you.

Even before we crash and burn, Jesus knows it's coming, and he has a plan to restore us. David put it this way in Psalm 139: 'I'm an open book to you; even from a distance, you know what I'm thinking. You know when I leave and when I get back; I'm never out of your sight. You know everything I'm going to say before I start the first sentence. I look behind me and you're there, then up ahead and you're there too—your reassuring presence, coming and going' (MSG).

David found that God is prepared for every eventuality of his life. God knew how David would react to every situation, when he'd thrive, and when he would fail. Jesus had the same knowledge of Peter, and that is true for all his disciples. But that knowledge is to our benefit, because as the Bible tells us in the book of Hebrews, in Jesus we have a High Priest who not only understands our problems with chaff—'For we do not have a high priest who is unable to empathise with our weaknesses, but we have one who has been tempted in every way, just as we are—yet he did not sin. Let us then approach God's throne of grace with confidence, so that we may receive mercy and find grace to help us in our time of need' (Hebrews 4:14–16)—but also is able to deliver us from it. 'Because Jesus lives forever, he has a permanent priesthood. Therefore he is able to save completely, those who come to God through him, because he always lives to intercede for them' (Hebrews 7:24–25).

And so, though we may fail, and like Paul in Romans 7, our faith may grow weary, Jesus's faith in us does not fail, and neither does his commitment and ability to truly transform us.

With Peter, Jesus covered him in prayer. And I know in my story, he did the same. David observed in Psalm 37 that though we may stumble, we will not fall, because the Lord helps us. This is what I found, what Peter found, and what countless disciples have found over the years. The only reason I crashed but didn't burn, that I stumbled but didn't fall, was because I had a High Priest who empathised with my weaknesses and kept praying that I would hold firm and find my way home. And when I did, I found God waiting with arms wide open.

The story of Peter's denial and restoration provides comfort for us in our weak moments, a comfort that the story doesn't end with our failure and our mistakes, that God's love is greater and his grace more than sufficient.

Throughout the Bible we see evidence of God working through people with far from perfect lives. The people God uses have 'interesting' backstories, to put it mildly. David had Bathsheba, Samson had Delilah, Elijah got scared, Moses got angry, Abraham lied, Rahab was promiscuous, Sarah laughed, John the Baptist doubted, Peter froze, and Solomon—where do we even start with Solomon? The list is a long one.

God is constantly calling broken people to join him in life.

And this is why only the broken are humble enough to surrender and why only the surrendered heart can be winnowed until all the chaff is brushed away. God wants us to understand that what he can do through us is not limited by our weaknesses, and there is a whole heap of stories to support that theory. Those whom God has called in the past, is calling in the present, and will call in the future are there as an example of the transforming power of his grace, a reminder to us that it is not by our might or power, but by his Spirit. The enemy may try to tell us we can't be the people God calls us to be because of the chaff within, but our God is greater than our chaff. Who we become is dependent on God's strength not ours, and his strenght has no limits. God is capable. The enemy doesn't get to win this battle. We can keep powering on in faith.

The story of our fall, just as with Peter's, doesn't have to be the final scene. It doesn't mean we are no longer 'useful' to God. Jesus charged Peter with these words: 'And when you have turned back, strengthen your brothers.'

With Peter having gone through a sifting process and emerging on the other side still standing, thanks to the unfailing grace Jesus provided, Jesus instructed Peter to go on and continue his mission. Carry on with your journey. Do not let that stumble deter you or give you any doubt. He says the same to us: 'Do not let any slip-up deter you from carrying out your mission.'

Paul put it this way in Philippians 3:13: 'Brothers, I do not consider that I have made it on my own. But one thing I do: forgetting what lies behind and straining forward to what lies ahead.'

The Devil will constantly look to remind us of the chaff he's found, but we must ignore him. Like Paul, we must press on towards what lies ahead. So keep your eyes on Jesus and continue with your mission, it's what he'd want us to do.

8

Join Me on the Mountain

(Matthew 17:1–13)

Not many of us know what we're supposed to do with the story of Jesus's transfiguration. We usually read it, scratch our heads, and move on. That's what I used to do anyway. But it is clearly a significant moment in Peter's journey. That day on the mountain, he saw Jesus for the first time in all his glory. Before this, he had believed Jesus was the Son of God; now he had seen it with his own eyes. Before he had only seen the earthly representation of the Messiah; now he saw his heavenly glory as well.

It must have been amazing.

Not only was Jesus present, but also two other greats were in their midst: Moses and Elijah. Moses, Elijah, and Jesus having a conversation. I am so curious to know what they were talking about, aren't you? And as if that were not mind-blowing enough, the apostles then heard the voice of God. And it confirmed what Peter had believed all along when the voice declared, 'This is my son, whom I love; with him I am well pleased. Listen to him!'

What an experience!

Mountaintop experiences in the Bible are usually remarkable ones. The mountaintop is a place where people have met with and experienced God in all his splendour, a place where their eyes were opened to see God in a way they never had before. Indeed before Peter and his mates experienced the Transfiguration, Moses and Elijah had their own mountaintop experiences during their time on earth.

In the case of Moses, he was quite a remarkable man, not just in terms of who he was and what he achieved, but particularly in the context of the relationship he had with God. You can find more details of that relationship in Exodus 19, 33, and 34, if you fancy some background reading. In any event, it is safe to say Moses's relationship with God is one I've always envied, and it's the kind of closeness I aspire to have. It is the very blueprint of what is possible when we search for God with all our hearts. Exodus 33:11 paints a brilliant picture of the depth of their relationship: 'The Lord would speak to Moses face to face, as one speaks to a friend.'

This relationship and closeness that Moses had with God was very much the driving force behind everything Moses did and the man he was. And it was a relationship built on the mountain. It was here, alone with God, that Moses was equipped to find himself and live a fulfilled life. The depth of the relationship he enjoyed was such that Moses's request for God to reveal his glory to him was not turned down (Exodus 33:18). No one had dared to make that request of God before, or indeed after Moses. It was generally believed that anyone who witnessed God's glory would die. But God agreed to reveal himself to Moses, hiding only his face.

'I will cause all my goodness to pass in front of you, and I will proclaim my name, the Lord, in your presence. I will have mercy on whom I will have mercy, and I will have compassion on whom I will have compassion' (Exodus 33:19).

Moses was a man who got to experience God at his powerful and glorious best. His journey was a remarkable one filled with signs and wonders, but it is his closeness with God that really stands out. Here is a man who was able to get God to change his mind regarding the Israelites on more than one occasion. His friendship with God was so deep that when he died, God took it upon himself to bury him in the same way you would bury someone you loved (Deuteronomy 34:5).

The good news is that in Jesus we are offered the same intimacy of relationship with God. But we have to want it, and we have to invest to get it. No relationship grows without a concerted effort to build a closeness with the other person. And Moses's relationship with God reached the level of intimacy it had because he committed to meeting God on the mountain. He committed to responding to God's invitation to join him there.

Elijah, another of the dudes who showed up at the Transfiguration, also had his own mountaintop experience, and you can follow his story in 1 Kings 18. In obedience to God, Elijah had declared there would be no rain in Israel for three years, and in the third year he received an invitation to meet with God on Mount Carmel. While there, he had a face-off with the prophets of Baal, the idol that had taken the place of God in the hearts and lives of the Israelites. Elijah came to an agreement with Baal's boys that they would each set up an altar, Elijah's to the Lord and the others' to Baal. Whichever deity lit up the sacrifice with fire was to be recognised as the one true God.

The prophets of Baal went first, with complete conviction that he would answer. They did all they could to get his attention. They screamed, prayed, danced, and even cut themselves. But Baal didn't show up.

Elijah got naughty and began to tease them. "Pray louder!" he said. "If Baal really is a god, maybe he is thinking, or busy, or traveling! Maybe he is sleeping, so you will have to wake him!"

In the end the Baal brigade gave up, and it was Elijah's turn. Suffice to say Elijah got an experience of God's power and presence, as in response to his prayer, God sent fire to the altar, even consuming the trenches of water around it. Elijah didn't need to scream and shout to get God's attention. He already had it—he was where God had called him to be after all. God didn't send only fire that day. In response to Elijah's prayers, he also sent rain to end a three-year drought.

Later in the gospel, James holds Elijah up as an example of the power of meeting God on the mountain: 'Elijah was a human being just like us. He prayed that it would not rain, and it did not rain on the land for three and a half years! Then Elijah prayed again, and the rain came down from the sky, and the land produced crops again' (James 5:17).

James is keen to stress that Elijah is 'just like us'. Many times we look at people like Moses and Elijah like they were X-Men with superpowers. But they were just people like us, with gifts and abilities just like we have gifts and abilities. The reason they lived such fulfilled lives filled with experiences of God's power, the reason they had the depth of relationship with God where they could see, hear, and be moved by him, is because they invested in meeting God, in responding to his invitation. When he called, they answered.

If you haven't figured it out by now, the mountain is a place of prayer, a place where we move away from everything else to be with God. And being in the presence of God is no less remarkable now than it was in the days of Moses and Elijah.

It is such a special place, and one that is by invitation only.

It was God who gave the invitation to come both to Moses and to Elijah. In the story of Moses in particular, no one else was permitted to the mountain apart from him. And at the Transfiguration, it was Jesus who invited those four disciples to join him there. Seeing God in his glory is for special people only. And guess what, that's exactly what you are.

In Jesus, God makes the invitation to come and meet him at the summit, and Jesus's offer in Matthew 11:28—'Come to me, all of you who are weary and carry heavy burdens, and I will give you rest'—is just one of many invitations that Jesus makes to us to join him on the mountain, the most symbolic of which was when the curtain of the sanctuary that separated God from common folk was torn into two at Jesus's death as a declaration from God that all who believed were now welcomed into his presence. As the writer of the book of Hebrews put it, 'Therefore brothers and sisters, we have confidence to enter the most Holy place, by the blood of Jesus' (Hebrews 10:9).

You and I, as disciples of Jesus, have been called into the presence of God. We have been invited to the mountaintop. Yet not many of us go there, and I think the main reason for this is that we do not recognise how powerful a place it is.

This lack of recognition means we end up treating the sacred as ordinary.

When Moses first meets God at the burning bush, he is told to take off his shoes because he is standing on holy ground, stepping on the very same surface that God has walked on, and the sight of God coming to speak with Moses was an awesome spectacle for the Israelites. God still comes to us in the same way. But because the gift of grace was given to us so freely, we sometimes take it for granted. How often do we come into God's presence without the slightest awe or expectancy?

We can be like Cain in the Bible, who comes to meet God with a token gesture. For him it is just another obligation to fulfil. He is not fully present in what he is part of. His brother Abel, on the other hand, is fully aware of the great privilege of having God's undivided attention. He goes to meet God with a full representation of what is going on in his life. He gives that time with God the best he's got to offer. The contrast between the two is indicative of the response they get from their time with God. Abel goes with an expectant heart, an acknowledgement of who it is he is going to be with; Cain treats it as a routine, a tick in the box. The result? 'The Lord looked with favour on Abel and his offering, but on Cain and his offering he did not look with favour' (Genesis 4:4–5).

It's easy, like Cain, for us to begin to see prayer as just another 'thing to do', because what prayer is has been lost on so many of us. For years it has been misrepresented and undersold as another avenue to receive what we need in life. And so what usually happens is, if we've got a plan in place to meet that need, and if there is a clear path leading from here to there, prayer doesn't seem so important. It becomes a case of 'I don't need to go to the mountain; I've got Baal.'

And so we end up on the mountain only when the road gets tough. But those who truly walked with God made sure they kept the prayer line open at all times. It was David who shared these amazing words from Psalm 116: 'I love the Lord because he hears my voice and my prayer for mercy. Because he bends down to listen, I will pray as long as I have breath.'

Being with God in prayer, wherever your mountaintop may be, having the undivided attention of the King of Glory himself, is not something to be treated lightly. Far from being a chore, it is an opportunity, an opportunity to have our eyes open to see God—and it is some sight. There is so much of God to see, know, and understand, and catching a glimpse of our heavenly Father in a new way is one of the most satisfying experiences, if not the most satisfying experience, anyone could have. Whether he is revealing his name in a new way or is answering by fire, it is not to be missed.

The place of prayer is also where we discover our purpose in life. Not only does God reveal himself to us, he also opens our eyes to who we are called to be. Moses, Elijah, Samuel, Isaiah, and many more discovered their purpose in life during a conversation with God, and the same is available to all his disciples.

The truth is that only the Creator truly knows why you were created; only the one who called you knows why you were called; and only the one who chose you knows why you were chosen. The answers to these questions are so precious that Jesus died to give you access to them. That tells me that they are answers worth knowing. It also tells me that when God called us his masterpiece and treasure, he wasn't kidding around. The world tries to suggest different ideas and images that we should pursue and live for, and sometimes we think we know the best path for our lives, but in reality only the Creator truly has the answers to the question 'Why am I here?'

We find those answers in his presence.

Some travel around the world to find themselves. We only need to respond to his invitation to sit with him on the mountaintop. I always envied Moses's relationship with God, but every time I thought to myself, *Why can't I have that?*, a voice was always quick to reply, 'You can, and you do.'

Jesus bought us a lifetime supply of face time with the living God, the same kind Moses and Elijah had, the same kind Peter and his mates had. All we need to do is accept the invitation and, like Abel, treat that time with God as the sacred treasure that it is.

Too often though, like the Israelites, we turn to a Baal-type figure for answers. We turn to Baal to reveal his glory and tell us who we are. The glory of a career, status, or pleasure can seem so amazing to behold and appear to be a good identity to define ourselves by, so sometimes it may seem like Baal is delivering. But as the Israelites found, when the time of drought comes, there is only one God who is capable of sending rain. And when we truly need answers, when we need a God who can step up, only one has the power to answer with fire.

Baal, in the end, is, quite frankly, a pathetic substitute for God. No one is quite like Jehovah.

Another thing to bear in mind is how these mountaintop experiences should impact our day-to-day lives. Moses, upon leaving God's presence, used to glow so brightly, the people were afraid to look at him. And being with God should have the same effect on us; it should make us shine. Jesus spoke about our light shining so bright that it empowers us to do good in our world, impacting it in such a way that brings God glory. This is what being with God does for us.

But it can be all too easy for the world to have more of an impact on us than our time with God does on the world. This was something Moses experienced first-hand.

He had just been with God for a considerable length of time, and on his return to the Israelite camp, he found the Israelites worshipping a blinged-up goat. And they were not just worshipping this jewellery-ridden mammal; they were also crediting it with their salvation from Egypt, as well as engaging in acts of debauchery. Moses completely lost it.

He had come down from the mountain with two tablets in his hands upon which God had handwritten his covenant with the people. Their own invitation to the mountain. Moses, in his rage, forgot what he had in his hand and thrashed the tablets into the ground, smashing them to pieces.

These precious tablets, a handwritten invitation from God to his people, that Moses had spent considerable time with God to obtain, were smashed to pieces in a moment of rage. And we have all been there.

It is so easy to lose focus and be distracted by the same old temptations the moment we descend from the mountain and get back into life. It is so easy to end up being riled up by the same old things.

How often do we end up smashing the sacred tablets that God has placed in our hands because life got stressful?

Elijah was no different. Once he descended from the mountain, he gave into his fears. God had just given him a great victory. He had answered Elijah's call with fire, sent rain, and given him the power to run quicker that Usain Bolt on steroids. Still, when Jezebel threatened to find and kill him, Elijah got scared and ran. Did he not think the God who answered by fire was capable of delivering him from Jezebel?

How often do we allow our fears to swallow up the reassurance we receive from God in prayer? How often do our fears make us forget all our previous mountaintop experiences and the many ways God answered with rain and fire, the many times he gave us strength beyond our means?

And Peter? Even after seeing Jesus in all his glory on the mountain, even after being told that the Messiah must die but will come back to life, when events began to unfold, he panicked. He denied Jesus and, along with the other disciples, abandoned his Lord and went into hiding. He forgot all about Moses and Elijah on the mountaintop. He forgot all he learnt and all that was revealed.

We look at these men like they had supernatural powers, but when we take time to study their lives, we discover that they were just like us. They too got scared, they too denied Jesus, and they too smashed covenants. Life has a tendency to make us forget what God has done. It's no coincidence then that Jesus purposely initiated the Lord's Supper so that we would remember him.

So how do we ensure our time with God has a lasting effect on how we do life? We keep going back. This is exactly what Moses, Elijah, and Peter did. This is what we must do as well.

God does not shut the door to us when we fail. Whether we've given into fears or other emotions, whether we've denied him or broken sacred convents, thanks to the grace Jesus provides, the door to us remains open. The invitation to the mountaintop is a permanent one.

Moses returned to the mountain, and God met with him again. He received a new set of tablets and left the mountain with his face reflecting the glory of God. He was empowered to be light again. Elijah returned to the mountain, and God comforted, encouraged, and then retired him with a first-class ticket to heaven. Elijah didn't die; he just got on his chariot and went off to an eternal mountain to meet the King he had served so well.

And Peter, he met Jesus on the mountain and received his commission again: 'Go into all the nations and make more disciples, teaching them what I've taught you.'

And with it came these words of affirmation and acceptance: 'And surely I am with you always, to the very end of the age' (Matthew 28:20).

And us?

Well, why don't you go up to the mountain and find out?

9

Moving Mountains

(Mark 11:12–23)

Still on the topic of mountains, the story here begins with a rather bizarre incident. Jesus, within earshot of his disciples, curses a fig tree because it had no fruit. Thing is, it wasn't even fig season. Surely that was a little harsh on the tree. The next day as they walked past said tree, Peter found that the tree was completely withered.

What is going on here?

Jesus was known to use the analogy of a tree and its fruit to teach his disciples about what following him looked like. In John 15:5, he made this comparison: 'I am the vine; you are the branches. If you remain in me and I in you, you will bear much fruit; apart from me you can do nothing.'

Two key messages here. First, we are to bear fruit, and second, we do that when we remain connected to Jesus. Let's consider these words in connection to the fig tree. The tree had no fruit to give because it wasn't fig season, so when Jesus came to it, it had nothing to offer him. This is a picture of what happens when our discipleship is seasonal. Sometimes we are less available to Jesus than we should be, and our investment in our discipleship is dependent on the season of life we're in. Other things get in the way, and so when Jesus shows up, desiring to use us in the work he is doing, we've got nothing to offer him. We haven't stayed connected and we haven't been available, so we have no fruit.

In Galatians 5, Paul lists the fruits of the Holy Spirit as love, joy, peace, patience, kindness, goodness, faithfulness, gentleness, and self-control. When Jesus comes knocking at our door, these are the fruits that he is hoping to find developed within us. Do we have love to give or maybe a bit of kindness? Can we be faithful or have self-control? We are the vessels through which Jesus heals our world. We are his hands and feet. But when he comes to our branch, will he find fruits that he can work with?

There can be a certain seasonality attached to the development of the fruits of the Spirit.

For some of us, we thrive the most in difficult periods. We respond to the tough times by drawing closer to God and investing ourselves more into his presence because we need him to pull us through. In those moments, as we abide in Christ and him in us, we find that we are more fruitful. The Spirit is at work and growing those seeds within us because we are more available to him. However, the moment it's plain sailing again, we drop our guard and are not as invested in being available to God; we go into off season.

For others it works in the opposite direction. We are available and thriving in the good times and lashing out and barren once things get tough. And so it is no surprise, given a seasonal response to discipleship, that on many occasions it is the opposite of the fruits of the Spirit that are developing in our lives. Rather than joy, there is dissatisfaction. Resentment replaces love, and anxiety drowns out peace. So when Jesus comes around with a hunger we can feed, we are in no position to help out. We can't say, 'Here am I; send me,' because we are in no position to go anywhere.

Wherever we find ourselves on our journey, God has placed us there strategically. It is no accident. He has placed us there because he has invested in us all we need to bring light to the dark places in our environment. That is why God's main focus is on who we are becoming. If we fail to understand who we are and grow into our bodies, we will be like that fig tree and fig season will never come round.

In the parable of the weeds in Matthew 13, Jesus speaks about how the people of the kingdom of God are spread across the earth to carry out God's work of bringing life to it. However, just as Jesus is planting the people of the kingdom, the enemy is planting weeds. The enemy is putting things in our path that can trip us up and entangle us. And sometimes we get so entangled in the weeds that our light becomes darkness. This is where we find that the fruits we are producing aren't those that give life to us or others. If anything, they have the complete opposite effect.

The test for any disciple in terms of our development is this; when Jesus comes to us, do we have any fruits to offer him?

We can study the Bible every second, sit on the mountaintop all day, and never leave the church building. But if those experiences and practices are not making us more fruitful, if we are not seeing the fruits of the Spirit growing and developing in our lives, and if we are not equipped to feed our Lord when he is hungry, then we are doing something wrong.

Jesus tells us that outside of him, we can do nothing, but if we remain in him and he in us, then we will bear much fruit.

How do we do that?

As the story continues, the disciples join Jesus on his trip to the temple, and when he gets there, he gets very angry. There are people using the place of worship for selfish gain, treating the sacred as worthless, and Jesus is not having that.

'My house will be called a place of prayer for all nations, but you have made it a den of thieves.' And with those words he drives them out of the temple. Having grown up to Bible pictures of a slim, blue-eyed boy with the face of an angel, I find it hard to picture Jesus chasing a group of able-bodied men out of the temple all by himself, but this is pretty much what he does.

Why is he so mad?

Jesus is taking a stand against the things that stand in the way of people establishing a true connection with God, namely the distractions that have been created and the complete disregard for the purpose of the temple. It was a place that was meant to house the presence of God and bring healing to many. Instead it had become a place where people got robbed. The place that was meant to give abundant life had become a location for stealing, killing, and destroying.

In 1 Corinthians 6:19, Paul refers to our bodies as the temple of the Holy Spirit. In other words, our bodies are God's dwelling place. So listen to Jesus's words again in that context: 'Your body will be called a place of prayer for the nations.'

We are called to be people who are not only connected to God but also serve as vessels that connect the nations to him as well. We are vessels for light. When people come into contact with us, they are meant to come into contact with abundant life. But when Jesus comes visiting our temple, what will he find, a place of prayer or a den of thieves?

In John 10, Jesus refers to the enemy as someone who comes to steal, kill, and destroy. This is his very purpose in life. While Jesus comes to give us abundant life, the Devil plants his weeds, intent on killing our dreams, stealing our joy, and destroying our future. He does this in the main by making sure those fruits fail to develop. He plants weeds in our lives that get in the way of growing fruit, and so our temple becomes a den of thieves.

We look in the spiritual mirror and see too little joy or insufficient self-control. As a result, we ask ourselves, *What is going on?*

We need a Saviour, the kind who comes in and drives away all the things that get in the way of our temple being a place of prayer.

Hallelujah—we have that Saviour.

He comes into our lives and begins to highlight where the thief has set his stall. He calls us out on where the weeds have been sown and helps us to pull them out. He cleanses us with his blood and aggressively drives out the habits, attitudes, and beliefs that hinder us from being fruitful. But for Jesus to do this work in our lives, we have to be in a place where we recognise that the work needs to be done.

In Revelation 3:16, Jesus has these words for one of the churches: 'Because you are lukewarm—neither hot nor cold—I am about to spit you out of my mouth.'

The problem with the lukewarm disciple is that his/her life gets stale and barren, and there is no recognition of this. When we're hot, we are thriving; when we're cold, we recognise that something is wrong and so are more likely to go running back to Jesus to help us be fruitful again. But when we are lukewarm, we're slowly walking into death, just like the fig tree.

The biggest danger to the church is lukewarm Christianity—it is the epitome of an unfruitful and barren life. A life that accepts being without fruit, one that views seasonality as normal.

We must guard against sleepwalking into death.

As Jesus and the apostles leave the temple, they come across the withered fig tree, which Peter points out to his Lord. Jesus responds to him with these words: 'Have faith in God and truly I tell you, if anyone says to this mountain, Go and throw yourself into the sea, and does not doubt in their heart, but believes that what they say will happen, it will be done for them.'

In other words, there is nothing that God cannot achieve through us once we push on in faith. If we will follow Jesus's counsel to seek after God's kingdom, if we are always in season, then there is no limit to how far God can take us. There isn't a mountain on earth that can get in our way. If we will invest in growing as disciples of Jesus, in being fruitful disciples who believe in God's purpose for our lives, then we will find we are living the kind of life and having the kind of faith that is unstoppable.

We often stop abiding in Christ when we are distracted by life. It's easy to focus on Jesus when it's fig season. Or at least that is what we think. We tell ourselves that when that season comes, we'll be more available and connected, that right now, there are other things we need to pursue. We have our own hunger and thirsts to quench, and we don't have the time to do things for others, even if the other is Jesus. But a faith that believes in God as the one source through which every hunger and thirst is satisfied and through whom every need is met is released to keep our eyes firmly where they belong.

And so when the weeds come, when the Devil tries to sow anxiety to take the place of peace, or lust to replace self-control; when he tries to offer resentment instead of love or the option of aggression over kindness; when the Devil brings his mountain of weeds; we can command it to get away from us and drown in the sea. Nothing will get in the way of our walk with God.

It was James who coined the phrase 'Faith without works is dead.'

It is not enough to say we have faith; we must live that faith out. If we believe that God is in control and has his eyes on us and ours, then we fight back against the temptation to worry by being a source of joy and peace to someone in need. We show our faith in God's goodness by being kind-hearted and gentle people. We show our faith in Christ's calling over our lives by pressing on with an endeavour to become ourselves. We show our faith by spending time with God in prayer to discover who he is and who we are, and being that person in our day-to-day lives.

The faith that moves mountains is the type of faith that is built through a life that abides in Christ, a life that stays connected to him and that lives out what it believes by bearing fruit. The faith that moves mountains arises from a life that practises love and joy, a life that dares to believe in the power of God within us to resist the advances of the enemy, a life that doesn't give in to the mountain but tells it to move.

So stay fruitful, because we can be sure of this, the time will come when Jesus shows up at our tree.

10

Carrying Crosses

(Matthew 16:21–27)

Ever feel like God is leaving you in the dark about certain things, like you don't have a clear idea on how a particular journey is meant to pan out? I definitely do.

Many times I find myself wishing that God would just reveal the full picture of what is going on, that he would tell me exactly what his plan is—the when, what, and why—and that he would let me in on when stuff is going to happen, how it's going to happen, and through what means. That he'd just come to me in a dream or something and say, 'ND, do this in this way and at this time.' I feel like if he did then I wouldn't worry or panic about things, that I'd just go with the flow.

Ever feel the same?

Peter, like us, probably wanted to be in the know as well, but when he got his wish, he didn't like what he heard. When Jesus debriefs his disciples of events to come, including his crucifixion and death, Peter's response was to pull him aside and give him a stern telling-off: 'Never Lord,' he said. 'This shall never happen to you!'

I've since learnt that no matter how tempting it is to want to know the full picture, sometimes it's in our best interests that we don't. I wonder what those who've gone before us would have done if presented with the full picture of events to come. Would David have signed up for a good chunk of his life spent running away from a crazy king? Would Joseph have signed up for slavery and time in prison on trumped-up rape charges? Would Elijah have signed up for Jezebel?

I guess we'll never know.

We desire for all to be revealed because we like to have an element of control over our destiny. It's a sense that says, *If I know what to expect, then I'm in control. If I know what lies at the end of each road, then I can choose— then I'm in charge.* Eve wanted the freedom to be in control, to have all knowledge. It sounds so appealing at first, but then when the Garden of Eden was traded for the world we have today, a world where humankind battles for control, she soon found out control is not all it's cut out to be.

As disciples, we are called to follow, not lead. We already made a choice, and that choice was to follow Jesus, to take the red pill. That choice means that we trust in the knowledge that Jesus is in control and that he knows where each path leads. We trust in his Word, where he assures us, 'I will guide you along the best pathway for your life. I will advise you and watch over you' (Psalm 32:8).

We take peace in those words and follow him. Even when it leads to the cross.

I don't know about you, but I have never liked the idea of carrying the cross. When I initially came to faith in Jesus, I hoped it would mean a life full of only beautiful moments. As far as I was concerned, God loved me completely and could do anything, so I put two and two together and figured I had signed up for a life of never-ending bliss. It wasn't long before I realised I had gotten it wrong.

Like Peter, I have pulled Jesus aside in prayer many times and given him a piece of my mind. Why was he leading me down this completely undesirable path? And why was the cross so heavy?

And, as it was to Peter, Jesus's response to me was this: 'You do not have in mind the concerns of God, but merely human concerns.'

Thankfully he spared me the 'Satan' reference.

When I think of it, my biggest frustration with the cross is that it inconveniences me. I am often more inclined to obsess over how the journey hurts me than to hope in how God will use it to heal. Right from the fall in the Garden of Eden, we have been programmed to worry more about human concerns than heavenly ones. We want what we want, and the world around us is quick to applaud that as a good quality. So when the path is not a bed of roses, we doubt the wisdom of God or his presence with us in it.

Peter, like the other disciples, was expecting Jesus to establish a kingdom like the ones he saw around him, one that was focused on the glory, wealth, and fame of the individual. Jesus calls us to a different kind of kingdom, one that heals the broken and brings light to the dark places, one that restores hope where there is bitterness, and peace where there is pain. And Jesus warns about the travails of pursuing an earthly kingdom: 'Do not store up for yourselves treasures on earth, where moths and vermin destroy, and where thieves break in and steal. But store up for yourselves treasures in heaven, where moths and vermin do not destroy, and where thieves do not break in and steal. For where your treasure is, there your heart will be also' (Matthew 6:19–21).

Sometimes we are so focused on earthly kingdoms, we lose sight of the heavenly one. However, Jesus is clear that because of the brokenness of the world, the treasures that we can build for ourselves here are at best temporal, and placing hope in them will lead to disappointment. He calls us to be part of something much bigger, to be part of the journey of bringing God's kingdom to earth.

But sometimes there is a disconnect between us and God, and this happens because while we are focused on the how, the when, and the why, he is focused on the who. His greatest interest is who we are becoming. That is his biggest commitment to us. God's desire is that we become ourselves, that we discover the person he has equipped us to become, that we unwrap each layer of our personality, gifting, talent, passions, interest, and story until the fullness of life that Jesus intends for us is fully revealed.

He understands that without this, we will fail to live fulfilled lives. And if we do not live fulfilled lives, it is not just we who suffer; all those whom we have been commissioned to bless miss out as well. The world gets a bit darker whenever one of God's lights fails to shine.

God is committed to helping us shine.

But to discover who we are, we need to be willing to let go of the ideas and perceptions we've held before. And this is where we struggle. Letting go of our own dreams, interests, and desires to take up those that God gives us is where we often fall short. Like Peter, we may have imagined a kingdom on earth, and we see God's plan as one that 'gets in the way'.

But hear Jesus's words again: 'What good will it be for someone to gain the whole world, yet forfeit their soul' (Matthew 16:26)?

We could gain all the kingdoms of this world, but if we never discover who we are, we have not really lived. There will always be that question that forever stays with us. To spend our lives dominated by human concerns is to never experience life. In the end when we hold on and refuse to let go, we are losing rather than gaining. Nothing that is given to God is ever lost, and nothing that is kept from God is ever safe.

Sometimes the cross seems heavy. There are times when the path that God chooses for us does not look great, but that is where trust and obedience comes in.

When I was younger, we watched this detective series about a maverick cop called Sledge Hammer, who often didn't follow the conventional way of doing things. Whenever his colleagues would get alarmed about his approach to a particular case, he would reassure them with these words: 'Trust me, I know what I'm doing.'

The same applies to our walk with Jesus.

Surely there were times when David, Moses, and Joseph, to name a few, wondered what was going on. Peter definitely was aghast at the change of tack Jesus was suggesting. But God has promised not only to guide us on the best path but also to advise and watch over us. He knows what he's doing. In Jeremiah 29:11, he shares these words: 'I know what I'm doing. I have it all planned out—plans to take care of you, not abandon you, plans to give you the future you hope for.'

The cross may be heavy, but God knows what he is doing. At best, we have an idea of what path is best for us, but God knows what it is and is committed to taking us there. But to experience that path, we need to let go of whatever it is we're holding unto and let God have our hands instead. Moses had to put down his staff, and Peter his net, to follow Jesus. What do you have to put down? What earthly kingdom so has your buy-in that you cannot let it go in pursuit of the heavenly one?

Hebrews 11 talks about faith as believing that a life spent seeking after God is the most rewarding way to live. This is cross-carrying faith, a faith that follows where the Saviour leads. It is a faith that faces the darkness and keeps shining, that is pricked by the brokenness of the world but keeps walking, that is shaken by the fear but keeps believing.

It is a faith that does not fear the cross, because it knows that we overcome it. The cross is but a stepping stone to resurrection.

Jesus carried his cross to bring salvation and healing to the world. He trusted his Father's plan, and he committed himself to seeking after God's kingdom rather than establishing one for himself on earth. Jesus understood that even if he had all of earth's glory (which he was indeed offered by the enemy), it would be worthless if he never became himself, if he never fulfilled his calling as the Saviour of the world.

We too are called on this journey of faith, this journey of following wherever the Saviour may lead. We too are called to trust in the treasures of God's kingdom over the pleasures of earthly ones. The treasures on earth often offer what they cannot deliver, things such as joy, peace, and rest, but often those pursuits end in disappointment and a strong sense of dissatisfaction.

When does giving the best of ourselves to worldly pursuits ever pay a dividend?

As part of the Sermon on the Mount, Jesus shares these words: 'Do not give dogs what is sacred; do not throw your pearls to pigs. If you do, they may trample them under their feet, and turn and tear you to pieces' (Matthew 7:6).

Many times we give the best of us to pursuits that are not worth it. The best of our time, our dreams, and our finances goes towards establishing earthly kingdoms that in the end turn around and hurt us. How often have hopes, dreams, and relationships been trampled on by the pigs of an earthly kingdom?

Does it not make more sense to trust our best with the one who loves us so much he died for us, to trust in the leadership of one who is committed to helping us discover who we really are?

The narrow path is often the less desired one because there's a cross there somewhere, but fear not, after the cross comes resurrection. Keep following your Master. You'll be glad you did.

11

Heal the World

(Mark 5:21–43; Acts 9:32–43)

In Mark 5 we read about two hopeless situations where interaction with Jesus led to healing and life. First up is the woman with the issue of blood. She pressed her way through the crowd with a single-minded belief that if she could just touch Jesus's garment, the illness that had troubled her and baffled doctors would become a thing of the past. In the end her faith was not in vain, and she received her healing as well as a personal acknowledgement from Jesus, who interrupted a journey of great urgency to seek her out.

Then came the trip to Jairus's house. Jairus had approached Jesus to come quickly to his house because his daughter was ill, but before they arrived, they were met with some disturbing news: 'Your daughter is dead. Why bother the master anymore?'

I wonder how many times you've heard the message that a particular situation was beyond saving, that it was pointless to press on any longer, and that things were dead and buried. There's no point praying, and there's no point trying; it's dead. This is the same message Jairus and the woman with the issue of blood heard.

Jesus encouraged Jairus, 'Don't be afraid, just believe,' and they kept going.

When they finally arrived at Jairus's home, they found weeping and commotion there. Jairus's daughter by all accounts was dead, but not according to Jesus. His suggestion that she was only asleep was laughed at by the people.

It is good of Jairus to provide some comic relief at this very difficult time, they must have thought. But Jesus dismissed them, and taking Peter, James, and John, as well as the girl's parents, with him, he went to see the girl where she lay. He took her by the hands and, uttering, 'Talitha koum,' brought her back to life.

It was a bona fide miracle.

And while both events are remarkable on their own merit, what is equally important is the impact they had on Peter's life and journey.

In Acts 9:32–43, we see Peter carrying on Jesus's work on earth. First up, he brings healing to a paralysed man who had been bedridden for eight years. Just like Jesus before him, he brings life and healing to a situation that was desperate and hopeless. And then, in a manner very similar to Jesus with Jairus's daughter, he brings Dorcas back from the dead—another hopeless situation receiving healing from the power of Jesus via Peter.

Peter understood that it was his calling as a disciple to continue the work of his Master in bringing life and healing to his world. That same calling applies to every one of us who carries the title 'disciple of Jesus'. For everyone who makes the decision to follow Jesus, and that includes you and me, has been commissioned to be the kind of person who shines, heals, and gives life.

We are called to be people who do the things Jesus did while he was here, as Jesus himself points out in John 14:12, 'whoever believes in me will do the works I have been doing, and they will do even greater things than these because I am going to the father.'

It might seem a daunting task, but remember, Peter was a vulnerable, sin-filled fisherman when Jesus found him; he was far from perfect. But he went on to fulfil his calling as a disciple—and so can we.

When Jesus walked on the earth, what he was doing was modelling life to us. With every word he spoke, every sermon he preached, and every day he lived, he was showing us how to do life. Peter picked up on these lessons and applied them to his own life. We can find some examples of this in these stories.

To start with, Peter found that Jesus always made himself available, first to God and then to those who needed him. Making time to be with his Father was a familiar discipline that Jesus had, and on some of those occasions, he took Peter, James, and John with him. He modelled a life that paused to be with God. And that sense of always being available to God flowed through into his availability to others. Whether it was little children, blind beggars, lepers, or Pharisees coming for midnight visits, Jesus always made himself available. He was never too busy or too consumed in himself to be available to others. Take the woman with the issue of blood for instance. Jesus was making his way to Jairus's house. There was an urgency, a little girl's life hanging in the balance.

Yet he stopped.

He stopped to seek this woman out and acknowledge her. He recognised that something significant had happened in her life and that she needed to be acknowledged and affirmed. A big step of faith had been taken, and she needed to know it was recognised. So, he stopped and sought her out.

This story also shows how accessible Jesus was. He was a man of so much popularity and influence, a man in great demand wherever he went. His presence drew crowds in their thousands. Still he was always accessible and available to those who needed him. It is a quality he still has to date, one he modelled for Peter and indeed models for us.

Peter learnt that a disciple of Jesus should always be available to God and others. So, here's a first step for us. Most times we focus on what we don't have. We can be like the disciples when Jesus fed the five thousand, asking Jesus to send the people somewhere where their need could be met. We look at the size of the need, and comparing it to the size of our baskets, we don't think we have anything to offer. Jesus's reply: 'You feed them. You do something about it.'

One thing we can do is be available to those around us. Life can get really busy, and a lot of things place demands our time, but as disciples of Jesus, we are called to be more outwardly focused.

I grew up in Nigeria, and one of the biggest problems we faced growing up was with our power supply. There were constant power cuts, and sometimes we went months without any electricity. I found it a most exasperating experience. Even more frustrating, though, were those moments when the power came on but the current was so low that it couldn't light anything up. You would look at a light bulb, and it would literally just have a yellow dot in it. There was light, but it would almost have been better if there had been be nothing. The light did not produce life, and it did not shine. The power supply couldn't power anything; not the bulbs, or fans, or television sets, let alone a fridge or anything heavy. It was pointless. The dot served more as a reminder of what we were missing.

This is the kind of light we are at risk of being if we do not follow the example set by Jesus in being available, first to God and then to others. If we are not connected to God, then we, like the branch disconnected from the vine, have no power. We are just a dot in a lamp bulb; we do not give life to anything.

And if we are not people who are accessible, then we are like the lamp hidden under a basket that Jesus spoke about in Matthew 5. Again, we are unproductive and pointless. The purpose of light is to be visible, to shine, and to show the way to others. This is your purpose and mine, and the key to being this kind of light lies in always being available to do God's work in our lives and world.

As Jesus mentioned during his ministry, God is always at work. And wherever we are, you can be sure that God is trying to involve you in the work he is doing there. He is constantly prompting in a particular direction, towards a need he has equipped us to meet or a life he has empowered us to heal. But if we are closed up and unavailable, we will miss out on the things he is trying to show us. Paul writes in Ephesians 5:15–16: 'Be careful, then, how you live—not as unwise but as wise, making the most of every opportunity, because the days are evil.'

Jesus, in his parable about the builders, spoke about the foolish man building his house on the sand, and aligned that illustration to those who hear his Word and do not put it into practice. Just before this parable, he had spoken about what it means to be a true disciple, saying that it is not about words but about acts of obedience, 'doing the will of his Father'. And God's will is that we make ourselves available for the work he is doing to restore the world and that we seek after his kingdom. As Paul noted, in these evil days where the darkness can be fierce, Jesus requires the light of his disciples to shine bright.

So we must stay in close proximity to our Saviour, abiding in him and him in us. This is how we get to live fruitful lives. This is what Peter does, and as a result he receives the power he needs to become himself. He would later write these words: 'His divine power has given us everything we need for a godly life through our knowledge of him who called us by his own glory and goodness' (2 Peter 1:3).

Next thing Peter learnt was to be vigilant, to be fully present. When Jesus takes Peter with him to Jairus's daughter's room, it is preparation for what Jesus would have Peter do later on. It is a teachable moment, a 'this is what you do in these situations' type of work experience. If Peter hadn't been observing diligently, if he hadn't been fully present as he walked with Jesus, he would have been like those Jesus spoke about when he said, 'Though seeing, they do not see; though hearing, they do not hear or understand' (Matthew 13:13).

As we walk with Jesus, he wants to open our eyes so that we may see what he is doing in our world and where he is calling us to join him. When we see God at work, or when our hearts are stirred to notice a need or a brokenness in our midst, it is God prompting us. It is his Spirit waking us up from our slumber and saying, 'Arise, disciple of the Most High. Arise and become yourself!'

In many ways we are like the garment that the woman reached for in Mark 5. For a lot of people, we are their only connection to Jesus. Like the clothes Jesus wore that day, when the world comes into contact with us, the power of God should be released from us into their lives—the power of his love and grace, the power of his healing and mercy, the power of the truth that sets free. There are many in our world reaching out for an experience of God's healing grace, but if we are too busy in ourselves, how are we ever going to see them?

There is a hopelessness and desperation in our world that God sees. He has equipped us to be the answer to it, but are we seeing what he is showing us, and are we listening when he is leading us?

The first steps are to be available and fully present to and with God. God is not necessarily looking for people who are perfect, who have 'free time', or who have all the answers. God is looking for people who will make themselves available to him, who are willing to see what he is showing them, and who are open to follow where he is leading them. I pray that by his amazing grace we become those people.

The next step is to give what we have. God never asks for what we do not have. To Moses in Exodus 4:2, the question was 'What is in your hand?' It is the same question he asks us today. Moses had his staff, David his sling and bow, the boy his bread and fish. Everyone has something. The problem is that we often think that what is in our hands can't achieve much, that it is too little and too unspectacular to make a difference to anyone. We let ourselves be convinced that we have neither the power nor the ability to make a difference. We certainly can't heal or bring the dead back to life like Peter did. We end up seeing God through the eyes of our own limitations, and as a result, we don't really push forward in faith, because we don't think it makes much difference whether or not we do.

But Peter, like Paul, as the latter shared in Ephesians 3:20, understood that God has given something unique to each and every one of us a gift, and that in addition he has given us his Spirit to work powerfully within us to achieve things beyond the sphere of our imagination. So when God brought Peter's attention to areas where there was hopelessness, Peter saw it as God wanting to bring hope into that situation through him, and he went for it. And when God brought his attention to areas where there was death, Peter saw it as God wanting to bring life through him, and so again he went for it.

Peter understood that this story was not about him or what he could achieve, but about God and what he desired to do. He understood from walking with Jesus that God's desire is to bring healing and life to our world, that he wanted this so badly, he was willing to give his life to make it a possibility. Peter understood that while God could do this directly, as he did in the person of Jesus, his love for us as his children means he wants to do this work with and through us. He wants us to be part of the work he is doing on earth. He wants to share the beautiful moments of life and restoration with us.

Peter understood that his role was to make himself available to God and then to offer what he had in faith. Nothing more, nothing less. It was then up to God to take what Peter had and do something amazing with it. God took Moses's shepherd staff and used it to bring deliverance to a nation. He took David's sling and stone and used it to bring down a giant. He took five loaves and two fish and used it to feed multitudes. And he took Peter's prayer and brought a woman back from the dead.

What have you given God lately?

All God requires is that we make ourselves available to him and offer what we have to the situations of despair and hopelessness that he draws our attention to; it is then up to him to do the rest. There are nations God wants to deliver, giants that he wants to take down, and multitudes whom he wants to feed through our story. So do not get bogged down by the number of loaves you have. If you sense a stirring in your heart to feed multitudes, then take those loaves to Jesus and let him figure out the rest. That is what we are called to do, to sense the stirring in our hearts, and to act upon it. To be available, fully present and ready to give in faith whatever it is that we have in our hands.

We are the garment; we are the prayer; we are the vessel through which God brings healing and life to our world. What an anointing. What a privilege. Glory be to his mighty and holy name.

12

My Precious

(Mark 10:17–27)

The story of Jesus and the man desiring to inherit eternal life is told in both Mark 10 and Matthew 19:16–30. The man in question had kept all the commandments and lived his life the way God had instructed, but he still felt like there was something missing. As he relayed these emotions to Jesus, our Saviour looked at him with deep affection, he knew where his problem lay.

'One thing you lack,' he said. 'Go, sell everything you have and give it to the poor, and you will have treasure in heaven. Then come, follow me.'

It proved to be too much to ask, and the man walked away disheartened, 'because he had great wealth'.

To understand what Jesus was getting at here, we need to reference something he said earlier: 'Where your treasure is, there your heart will be also' (Matthew 6:21).

We all have a treasure that defines us. It is that one thing that we base our worth on and that we look to for affirmation above all else. Sometimes we are not even aware of what it is, or that such a thing exists, until Jesus comes and puts a finger on it, just like he did in the life of the man in the passage. For that man, it was his wealth.

Any idea what it is for you?

For some of us that treasure is our career. For others it's a specific dream or goal, and for another it could lie in a relationship or some form of possession. Even as you read this, you probably know what yours is. I'll give you a clue: it's that thing you don't want to mention or think about, just in case God is listening.

The problems with these treasures is that, while they are not 'bad' per se, they have such an influence over us that they often end up dictating who we are. Jesus's message is that our relationship with God should be our biggest treasure. It should be the thing that defines and affirms us above all else. It should be the significant driver behind the person we are and are becoming.

Whatever owns our heart will drive our journey. And whatever we treasure the most will own our hearts. It will be the one thing we are willing to make the most sacrifices for and surrender our lives to.

If that treasure is found in God, then it becomes easier to surrender our dreams, desires, and aspirations to him, even when God suggests a change in direction. With God as our biggest treasure, we are more able to give up a script that has us as its central character in exchange for one that has us in a supporting role.

Because in the end, though the Devil sells us a script that claims to have us as the central figure, we are always playing a supporting role. The choice is to whom or what we play a supporting role to.

In the Garden of Eden, Eve was tricked into believing in a story that was all about her. But as she and Adam soon found, all they had done was replace a true treasure for an artificial one. In the end they found themselves playing a supporting role to inferior treasures like status, possessions, and other material things—things incapable of giving life.

But we still pursue these treasures. They look nice and shiny; they look capable of giving us the life we always wanted and more. Jesus, however, teaches us that only the relationship we have with God, and a journey spent in unison with him, can truly give life. The writer of Hebrews put it this way: 'Whoever wants to please God must believe that a life spent following him is the most rewarding way to live.'

We see this belief in the life of Abraham, and it is no wonder he is called the father of faith. This is a man whose whole life seemed to be defined by a desire for a son, at least from the outside. He so longed for a son that even his names, Abram and Abraham, were wrapped around this identity, this hunger to be a father. Eventually after years of waiting, both before and after God's promise to him, he had his heir in Isaac.

And then God did the unthinkable.

One day he met Abraham with these words: 'Take your son, your only son, whom you love—Isaac—and go to the region of Moriah. Sacrifice him there as a burnt offering on a mountain I will show you.'

Talk about mountaintop invitations.

Abraham would have been fully entitled to react in the same way as the man in the passage in Mark's Gospel. He would have had far more reason to. After spending most of his life waiting for this son God had promised, he was now being asked to give him up just like that? But remarkably, Abraham followed God's instruction. No questions. He followed in obedience, just like that.

What a man.

For Abraham, his biggest treasure was his relationship with God, and that trumped everything else. So if following God meant letting go of other treasures, he was willing to go with it. He believed in God's love over his life and trusted in God's leadership not to steer him wrong. The writer of Hebrews referenced Abraham's faith in Hebrews 11: 'By faith Abraham, when God tested him, offered Isaac as a sacrifice. He who had embraced the promises was about to sacrifice his one and only son, even though God had said to him, "It is through Isaac that your offspring will be reckoned." Abraham reasoned that God could even raise the dead, and so in a manner of speaking he did receive Isaac back from death.'

In other words, Abraham trusted that God knew what he was doing. He so treasured who God was and his importance to the journey he was on that he was willing to follow him wherever he may have led.

And that is what your prime treasure does, it takes you places. There is nowhere we won't go for the pursuit of that which matters the most to us. We therefore have to be very careful what that is. We guard this treasure so carefully, holding it so close to our hearts, that it begins to control our every action and reaction. This is dangerous territory when that treasure is not God.

We are at risk of becoming like the character Gollum from the book *Lord of the Rings*. Gollum was so obsessed by this ring he had come into possession of that it came to define him. He looked to the ring for affirmation more than to anything else. He would stare at it and stroke it affectionately, repeating the words, 'My precious!' over and over again.

The ring dictated everything about him, his moods, his happiness, and his very purpose in life. Ultimately, in the end, it turned him into a monster.

This is why Jesus steers us from earthly treasures and points us towards heavenly ones. It is not for selfish reasons or because he wants to control or dictate to us; it is because he wants to save us from the dangers of earthly treasures.

We can either become ourselves or, like Gollum, become monsters. And the key to that lies in what owns our hearts.

I wonder what your 'precious' is?

I've had a few in my time: relationships, my football team, money, status, and the biggest one of all, the dreams that I carried from a young age. It didn't matter how many of the commandments I followed, something always felt missing because, primarily, the wrong thing was defining me; I had the wrong treasure.

Many times God would ask me to hand the ring over to him, and I have to confess my response was usually more Gollum than Abraham. I would snap, hiss, and then recoil into the corner of the room, stroking my treasure lovingly and declaring, 'My precious!'

I just couldn't bring myself to hand it over to God the way Abraham gave Isaac up.

The Holy Spirit is at work within us to help us see beyond ourselves, to help us understand that nothing given to Jesus is ever lost. But this work can never be complete while the treasure we value most is an earthly one. It is why Jesus's counsel to the man is to let go of his earthly treasure and follow him instead.

Jesus knew that this was what was holding the man back, and he offers us the same advice. But letting go is never easy.

Jesus went as far as to say that it would be easier for a camel to go through the eye of a needle than for the rich to enter the kingdom of God. And by this Jesus did not just mean wealth in monetary terms. I believe he was referring to all forms of material wealth. If we count our wealth in this life, if this is our focus, then experiencing God's kingdom will always be difficult. In fact, considering Jesus's illustration, it would be impossible.

If we value our wealth too much, we will never feel comfortable giving it away to make the world better for someone else. If our career means too much, we will continue in that organisation or that job even if it goes against everything we believe in. If that relationship or person is our everything, we will do whatever it takes to keep it, even if it means God and our faith suffer as a result. The more we are invested in this world, the wealthier we are, the more distant the kingdom gets.

Jesus shared these words in what is now referred to as the Beatitudes: 'Blessed are the poor in sprit, for theirs is the kingdom of God.'

For all who measure their wealth and worth in earthly terms, an experience of the kingdom of God is nigh impossible. But for those who measure their wealth in spiritual terms, who recognise the poverty of their spirit and the only wealth that matters, they inherit the kingdom of God.

This is what the man lacked, a shifting of focus as to what matters the most, as to what is more important. This is a place we all need to get to.

You see, when the treasure that defines us is our relationship with God, we live a life that is centred on protecting that relationship and growing deeper and deeper into it. Such a life experiences a peace that is not based on situations or circumstances, a joy that gives us strength to face whatever challenges come our way, and a faith that moves mountains.

A life spent in pursuit of this treasure also influences the way we treat those around us. We find ourselves striving to be more loving and forgiving because that is what our relationship with God demands. We find ourselves more interested in the needs of those around us because this is the path our treasure map leads us down. All in all, a life with God as our biggest and most definitive treasure, is a blessing both to us and to those who come our way.

It is light and salt, it is abundant life, and it is the kingdom of God.

Contrast that with a life centred on earthly treasures. In this picture, our mood, temperament, relationships, enthusiasm, and overall zest for life is dictated by how 'well' things are going and how bright the ring is shining. When it's in our hands and glowing brightly, we are happy and content. When it's not, we are grumpy and unapproachable.

A life centred on earthly treasures, whether that be a dream or a job or whatever, cannot experience God at his best, because such a life will always be held back from being completely released to God's grace. I have found in my own journey that a life centred on that ring leaves us suspicious and untrusting of the world around us. Everyone is trying to get our ring. We live life from the perspective of 'No one understands, no one is trustworthy; everyone just wants our precious.'

The person who lives that kind of life can never truly be a vessel of light and salt in the world, because how can someone be light when he or she is consumed by darkness?

Thankfully Jesus adds these words to his earlier statement about the challenges of experiencing God's kingdom: 'With man this is impossible, but not with God; all things are possible with God.'

To an extent, we are all Gollum. There is that something or someone that seems too shiny to resist, but because of the power of the Holy Spirit within us, it is possible to be transformed from Gollum to Abraham.

The Spirit opens our eyes to the futility of building treasures on earth and the importance of an eternal base. Perhaps he is at work now as you read, and you can hear God's voice calling you to put down the ring and follow him instead.

God comes to us with the invitation to let go of those things we've allowed to define us for so long and follow him. When we heed his call, we will find out that we actually haven't lost anything at all. In fact, we have gained more than we could have imagined. Rather than experiencing a setback, we have been put on the right track, rerouted from a path that would have created a monster to one where we become ourselves.

As Jesus reaffirms to Peter when he declares such a commitment, 'Truly I tell you, no one who has left home or brothers or sisters or mother or father or children or fields for me and the gospel will fail to receive a hundred times as much in this present age: homes, brothers, sisters, mothers, children and fields—along with persecutions—and in the age to come eternal life.'

All who let go of their earthly treasures for the sake of the kingdom gain a hundred times more in this life and in the one to come. Abraham did, as did Peter, as does everyone who chose to pursue the kingdom of God over the kingdoms we build on earth as human beings.

The question for us is, what treasure will we pursue?

When Jesus puts his finger on that area in our lives that we have allowed to define us more than anything else, when God asks us to stop 'Golluming' around and drop the ring, what will our response be?

Paul summarised it the best in Philippians 3, in words that have gone on to inspire many a song and prayer: 'I once thought these things were valuable, but now I consider them worthless because of what Christ has done. Yes, everything else is worthless when compared with the infinite value of knowing Christ Jesus my Lord. For his sake I have discarded everything else, counting it all as garbage, so that I could gain Christ and become one with him' (Philippians 3:7–9).

13

Talking Donkeys and Solitary Places

(Mark 1:35–39)

The story in Mark 1:35–39 was probably one of the first experiences the disciples had of Jesus finding time and space to be alone with God. Verse 35 tells us that he got up when it was still dark, left the house, and found a solitary place to pray.

The day before had been a busy one for Jesus, as most of the days in his ministry would turn out to be. He was involved in a lot of work, from healing Peter's mother-in-law to casting out demons. The whole town had gathered at the door to seek his help, and while Jesus was happy to give of himself completely to serve the needs of others, he never forgot where his strength came from.

Therefore, after a busy day of ministry, he recognised the need to recharge and knew that this would only happen if he was able to remove himself from everything and rest in the presence of his Father.

We often say we are too busy to find time to be alone with God, when the reality is that prayer exists *because life can get too busy*. It is because of the busyness of life that prayer, and in particular prayer in solitude, exists in the first place. Prayer is recognition that it is in God's presence that we find not only the rest we need, but also the strength to go again.

This was the case right from the beginning. In Genesis chapter three, we find God walking in the garden in search of Adam and Eve. God had placed Adam in the Garden of Eden to work and take care of it (Genesis 2:15), but God would show up in the garden to spend time with Adam. Why? Because Adam needed God's presence to renew his strength.

David declared in Psalm 16:11 that in the presence of God, there is fullness of joy. Nehemiah 8:10 tells us that the joy of the Lord is our strength.

The strength to go on comes from resting in God's presence, away from the noise of life.

Because if one thing is capable of drowning God's voice out, it is the noise we encounter every day. A million things compete for our attention. A million things call out to us, saying, 'Choose me! Focus on me! Worship me!'

It is difficult to pick out God's voice when we are in the centre of the noise. But when we pull away to be alone, to listen out for one singular voice, then God's voice triumphs above all else and we are able to hear him clearly.

Jesus was in a town where he was in demand. Everyone wanted a piece of him, his time, and his attention. He knew that if he was seen, he'd be dragged into another busy schedule. Did he mind? I don't think he did. He, however, understood the importance of running on the fuel of God's grace. It was either that or risking running on empty.

And if Jesus needed to recharge, so do we.

We have the tendency to power through our journeys in life without a moment's rest in God's presence. Jesus models a different way for us, and in Psalm 127, David shares these words of wisdom: 'Unless the Lord builds the house, its builders labour in vain. Unless the Lord watches over a city, the watchman stands awake in vain.'

One of the reasons we never stop is because we think that the success of the journey we are on depends on what we are able to do. Like Martha, we are oblivious to the opportunity to sit at the feet of Jesus, because this stuff isn't going to sort itself out. If we stop to rest, who's going to do the building or whatever it is we are trying to do? Who's going to build those dreams and watch over those interests while we are casting our gaze elsewhere?

But there is a better way, arriving at a place where we acknowledge who the most important watchman and builder is.

That it is all by his grace. Placing faith in God as our lead builder and watchman not only means we rearrange our priorities to make sure we are checking in with him but also facilitates a life of peace. When we are released from the burden of full responsibility over the house and city, when someone else who is extremely capable takes the lead, then we can find rest.

A realisation that God is the source of our strength and that it is by his power we are able to do all things will lead us into his presence. It will lead us to move away from the noise and the busyness of life and to find rest in him. Then we will be able to listen out for just one voice.

Because rest is not the only benefit of solitude. When we surrender to God's leadership and rest in his grace, he provides not only the strength to press forward but also guidance on which direction to go.

In the passage in Mark's Gospel, when Peter and the others finally find Jesus, he has a different course in mind. As morning comes round, the people of the town have flocked back to where Jesus was residing to seek him out, but he is not there. In response, Peter and the others go looking for him. But following the time spent alone with his Father, Jesus has been given a different path to follow.

'Let us go somewhere else—to the nearby villages—so I can preach there also. That is why I have come.'

You can never overestimate the importance of God's leadership and guidance. God declares in the words expressed in Psalm 32:8, 'I will instruct you and teach you in the way you should go; I will counsel you with my loving eye on you.'

These are such wonderful words that assure us of God's commitment to watch over us in order to see we are moving forward in the right direction and to give us his counsel. In life the noise can pull us this way and then that. We can get too cosy in our comfort zone, or we can get stuck in a rut or a bubble. In times of solitude, in that quiet space where we have our spirit tuned in for just one frequency, God's guidance becomes clear and our eyes are opened to the path that is not clearly obvious.

Many times we don't hear God's voice or experience his guidance because we are not expecting it. It is actually scary how often we go through life without expecting to hear from him. The truth is, God is always reaching out, always speaking to us, but his voice is often drowned out, sometimes by the noise of the world but other times simply by unbelief, a lack of faith.

And so when God does speak, either we are not listening or we explain it away by concluding it is something else. Sometimes God has to send a talking donkey our way to get our attention, as he did in the case of Balaam. In Numbers 22:21, we see the story of Balaam and his donkey. Balaam is about to go down a road that God is not pleased with, so an angel stands in the path to oppose him. Balaam's donkey's eyes are opened to see the angel, but Balaam cannot see it. He urges the donkey, which has stopped, to move forward, but it refuses and stays put. Balaam, in his frustration, begins to strike at his animal, and God opens the donkey's mouth. 'Am I not your own donkey which you have always ridden to this day? Have I been in the habit of doing this to you?'

It is then that Balaam's eyes are opened to see the angel before him, and his ears to hear his words: 'Why have you beaten your donkey these three times? I have come here to oppose you because your path is a reckless one before me.'

I wonder how many times God has had to send you a talking donkey to prevent you from going on a reckless path?

Maybe your 'talking donkey' was the car that didn't start, the job application that fell through, or the plans that didn't work out. Perhaps it is this book, though I'm not sure how I feel about being a 'talking donkey'.

When we are not listening or we can't hear him, God's commitment to us is such that he has to act all the same, for our own good. But this is not his preferred way of doing things. In Psalm 32:9 he says to us, 'Do not be like the horse or the mule, which have no understanding but must be controlled by bit and bridle or they will not come to you.'

Many times we are just like that. We pull away from God and the direction he's calling us. We're distracted by the house that needs to be built and the city that needs to be fortified. But when we remove ourselves to be with God in the quietness of solitude, our spirits are awakened to his voice again, and we no longer require talking donkeys.

In the silence, as we hear God speaking, we discover things we never understood before and paths we had never known existed. Sometimes we discover needs we never knew we had, as was the case with Adam. As Adam worked the earth and took care of animals and plants alike, God noticed from his time together with Adam that the latter was lonely. There was an Eve-shaped hole in his heart that God needed to fill. So God made Adam rest, and then he gave him Eve.

He desires to do the same for us.

We carry with us burdens of loneliness, fear, and worry, amongst other baggage, wherever we go, sometimes even without realising we're carrying them. But when we come to God, when we respond to Jesus's call to come and receive rest, it is then that those burdens are lifted and we are set free.

Whenever I find myself feeling down and I don't quite understand why, I know exactly where to go. I know that God understands. He knows the burdens, even those I can't quite see, and he is able to lift them and give me rest.

A busy life and schedule is never a reason not to pray; it is the very reason to pray. Prayer is a reminder of who is in control, in whose hands our lives are, and on whom our future actually depends. It is a time of rest, strength, and guidance.

But solitude does throw up another question, especially in the context of the story we were initially discussing. Why does Jesus go to be alone with God? Why doesn't he take his disciples along with him so they can pray together?

Well, because there is a time for corporate prayer, but it should never be instead of a time of solitude. It should be in addition to solitary prayer. In fact, one could argue that true corporate prayer is borne out of individual lives that are invested in times of solitude with God. The church, as Paul points out, is as good as the individual parts that make it up. If the arms and eyes, for example, are not doing what they should, then the body as a whole cannot function.

If the individual parts of Christ's body are not investing in time alone with God to seek his direction and leadership and to hear his voice, then there is no way the church will move in the right direction. It is just not possible.

Neither is it ideal to piggyback on someone else's experience of God, because while it is amazing to have someone pray for you, and while it is a great blessing to be gathered with others in prayer, nothing quite beats an experience of God for oneself. Nothing quite beats going to God in the middle of a difficult journey and experiencing his guidance through it. Nothing compares to building and watching with God.

Time spent alone with God does volumes for our relationship with him, just as quality time will do for any relationship.

The solitary place of prayer is not just a place for asking and receiving; it is a place where the real you meets with the real God. In any relationship, whether with a spouse or even a boss or colleague at work, one-to-one time is essential. It helps both parties involved in the journey to check that they are aligned and still heading in the same direction.

It is a place of confession and affirmation, a place to identify problems and offer solutions. It is a place to recognise sadness and sow the seeds of joy and fulfilment to press forward. Without that time, relationships fall away, becoming superficial and eventually nonexistent.

Without this space, relationships fail.

It is during a one-to-one that God calls out Adam's loneliness, and it's in a similar space that Jesus calls out Peter's pride. Don't miss the chance to experience God's calling out something you never knew was there. Because not only does he call it out, but also he takes steps to address and resolve it. God creates Eve for Adam, Jesus prays for Peter, and I too have experienced the blessing of God's insight and resolve.

Questions like 'Are you unhappy?' or 'Why are you so angry?' have caught me by surprise and drawn me back from the abyss I was threatening to fall into.

In that time alone with God, we can share every aspect of ourselves. Whether it's the deep darkness that no one wants to see or the worry that others find ridiculous, every part of us is welcome in that solitary place.

Because God doesn't just speak, he listens.

I love these words from David in Psalm 116:1: 'I love the Lord because he hears my prayers and answers them. Because he bends down and listens, I will pray as long as I breathe.'

The last sentence in particular gets me every time. David is saying, if God is listening, then I will keep speaking. As long as there is breath in my body I will pray, because God is listening.

Jesus pulls away to be alone with God because relationship matters, and a relationship is stronger when time is set aside to build it. In many ways, prayer is a journey. And if you've ever been in a relationship with someone, you'll know that going through a journey together often has an impact on the relationship in some shape or form.

Done properly, journeys are critical growing points in relationships. Whether that journey is raising children, working in a company, leading a ministry, or something else, those whom you make that journey with become important parts of your life. You grow together, and friendship, appreciation, and trust blossom as a result, especially with those who have remained by your side through difficult or significant periods.

Prayer has very much that same effect when done right.

In the place of solitude, we are vulnerable with God, and God in turn is vulnerable with us. We share our thoughts, hopes, and dreams with him in recognition that he may not agree with some or all of them. And he in turn shares his thoughts, hopes, and dreams with us, knowing that we may not agree with some or all of them.

My journey with God in prayer usually goes through the following stages:

- Stage 1—I come to God with my ideas and proposals, fully armed with reasons why they are the best ideas and why it would be incredibly silly not to go along with them.
- Stage 2—I get a sense that God doesn't quite agree with the brilliance of my ideas, and I become disappointed and sulky. Once I'm over that, I try harder to convince him to follow me on the road that I am determined to go down.
- Stage 3—God will not be convinced, so I reluctantly ask him to share his own plan with me. He obviously has one, given he's not agreeing to the quite brilliant one I proposed earlier.
- Stage 4—God slowly begins to reveal his plans to me, or at least the path he intends for me to go down. I am unsure. Hence begins another stage of proposals and counterproposals.
- Stage 5—I finally admit that I can trust God and I am called to follow him and not the other way round. I surrender my plans to God and let him know I'm available to him, wherever he may lead.
- Stage 6—I find rest.
- Stage 7—God leads me into life.

Through that journey, as I move from stage to stage, amidst the ups and downs and even in the fights and disagreements, I grow closer to God. I know him better, I understand him better, and he and I are better aligned. I discover things about him I didn't know and things about myself I wasn't aware of. Most importantly, at the end of it, I find myself in a place where finally I want what he wants, and that is the best place to be. It is a place of complete peace and rest, beyond what anything in this world can comprehend or offer.

For me these journeys have been priceless. I cannot imagine a life without that solitary place to have God's ear and attention, to hear his voice and receive his counsel. There is nothing in this life that is worth giving that up for. Absolutely nothing.

What Jesus modelled was clearly not lost on Peter either. He too came to recognise the importance of a solitary place, the importance of setting time aside to be alone with God, and he carried this discipline with him into his ministry. In Acts 10, we find him going up to the rooftop to pray. And there, he received guidance from God, guidance that showed him a better path to travel on, a path that, because of the noise around him, even within church life, he would have struggled to see clearly.

Just as he promised in the Psalms, God is still guiding us along the best paths for our lives. So, if life is busy, if you need strength, and if you're not sure which way to go, then don't settle for talking donkeys. Find a solitary place, and reach out to the one who watches over you and builds every aspect of your life. You'll be glad you did.

14

Drinking the Cup

(John 18:10–12)

One thing I have learnt about being a disciple is that it is more important to trust your leader than to understand him. I believe that in any relationship, trust is the most important ingredient. Everything dies if trust is broken or fails to exist. You can love someone, communicate with them, be honest, be available, and be faithful. You can do all these things and more. But if there is no trust between the two parties, then the relationship is bound to come a cropper.

I think this idea is very pertinent in our relationship with God, because there will be times when God is difficult to understand. There will be many moments when we can't quite see what he's seeing. He reveals as much in Isaiah 55:8–9: "'For my thoughts are not your thoughts, neither are your ways my ways,' declares the Lord. 'As the heavens are higher than the earth, so are my ways higher than your ways, and my thoughts than your thoughts.'"

The thing with God is that he can see way beyond our scope, and he understands things way beyond our reasoning. It is like when Samuel goes to anoint Israel's next king at Jesse's house. All David's family could see was a shepherd boy unworthy of an audience with Israel's finest, but God saw Israel's greatest king.

And was he right.

We cannot always see what he sees or reason like he reasons. We see shepherd boys; he sees kings. We see the cross; he sees the empty tomb. We see giants behind a mighty wall; he sees a land flowing with milk and honey. And that's where the disconnect comes between us and God at certain points in our journey, because while we see things from the 'us' and 'ours' perspective, God sees not only that but also the bigger picture.

And God's big picture is salvation for the world.

Above all else, God defines himself by his love, and that in simple terms means that who he is and everything he loves is driven by love—his love for his world, his love for us. In John 3:16 we hear that it was his love that led Jesus to come to die. And God's love has been inspiring events before and after the arrival of Jesus on earth.

But if who God is and everything he does is driven by his love for us, then why does he allow the suffering and pain that we encounter in life?

Sometimes the answers given, which I have found unsatisfactory, is that our expectation of God is wrong. I agree that sometimes we have the wrong idea of who God is. I've been there myself. Sometimes we are in this place where we treat God like a good-luck charm, but most times, especially as we move forward in our journey, such is not the case. Most times all we're asking is for God to be God.

We are looking for the loving Father, the ever-present brother, the all-conquering Saviour, the God whose every action and reaction is inspired by love, but sometimes he seems nowhere near. Why is that?

When Jesus was on earth, he intervened in every situation of hurt and pain that was brought to his attention. He interrupted funerals to bring people back to life, he healed lepers and stopped fevers, he fed crowds and cured medical ailments. As the Bible puts it, everywhere he went, he was doing good. Just as it was in the beginning, just as is God's plan, he was restoring the world to goodness and bringing light where previously darkness and emptiness existed. This is the Jesus that calls us to follow him, and this is the Jesus we expect to find on our journey, so I don't necessarily believe *expectation* is the problem, at least not in that sense.

What I've come to learn on my journey is to trust in who God is. Solomon, a man of immense wisdom, put it this way in Proverbs 3:5: 'Trust in the Lord with all your heart and lean not on your own understanding.'

And one day, as I lay in bed wondering where God was, I heard these words come to me, and a voice saying, 'Trust that God is good, and don't lean on your understanding of what God being good looks like.'

Those words woke me up. All this time I had been gauging God's goodness and love based on my understanding of what God being good and being love should look like in any particular situation. Now the words of Solomon came alive to me in a new way: trust that God is good and that he is love, regardless.

The enemy tries to change our view about who God is by getting us to see God from the perspective of our pain, viewing him from the lens of our hurts rather than viewing life from the lens of the one who is mighty to save us irrespective of the storms we encounter. And the reality is that in life there are difficult cups to drink, cups that don't always taste of the goodness of God that David spoke about in Psalm 34:8. And that is not out of some sadistic desire God has to get us to 'man up'; rather, it's because the world that we live in is broken.

And Jesus experienced that brokenness first-hand.

Peter is with Jesus in the Garden of Gethsemane, where Jesus is so cut up about what is about to happen that he sweats blood—an extreme case of stress. In a matter of moments, all the broken elements of the world will conspire against Jesus, leading to an unjust death. That night will see all the darkness of the world on display—greed, jealousy, lust for power, betrayal, injustice, wickedness, and many more vices—come to the fore, and Jesus is to endure all on his way to the grave. It is a difficult cup to drink, and so Jesus prays, 'Father, if you are willing, take this cup from me.'

I don't know about you, but I have definitely prayed this prayer a lot of times, a prayer begging God: 'Please don't make me go down this road, don't give me this cup—I don't want it.'

But Jesus understands that to be light, we have to confront darkness, and that to give life, we have to confront the places that are deprived of breath—even if that is death itself. And so he adds these words: 'Yet not my will, but yours be done.'

In the end, Jesus trusts in who God is. He trusts that his Father is good, that his Father is the very definition of love. If God is going to allow this cup, then that decision is being made based on God's great love and goodness. And while God does not take the cup away, he makes sure that Jesus has the strength to drink it. The strength that Jesus shows in the face of the darkness, all the way to the cross, is nothing short of remarkable. He was in human form and would have felt the physical and emotional pain in the same way that we would have, but what strength and resolve he showed to see it through to the end.

And this is what God does for us. He gives us the strength to face the difficult moments when we come into contact with the brokenness that exists around us.

But if you're anything like me, you'd just rather he gave a different cup. He is capable after all.

———

Joseph, another person who had a difficult cup to drink on his journey, learnt this lesson about drinking the cup, one he shared with his brothers when they were reunited: 'As for you, you meant evil against me, but God meant it for good, to bring it about that many people, should be kept alive, as they are today' (Genesis 50:20).

While the enemy looks to break us, God already knows about the darkness we are about to confront, and he has plans to ensure that rather than break us, we overcome and experience life for ourselves and others. Through the experience, God restores the world and us to the image he had intended from the beginning. Every time light confronts darkness, a part of the world is healed and a part of us is transformed into our true identity.

The alternative would be for God to hide us away from the world, to keep us wrapped up in cotton wool. But that would be in direct contradiction to who we are. We are light, and light is meant to shine; we are salt, and salt is meant to be used. For light to shine, it must face darkness, and for salt to add flavour, it must confront bitterness. For disciples of Jesus to thrive, we cannot stay hidden from what is out there. We will have to face it head-on and overcome, just as our Saviour did.

Drinking this particular cup was part of Jesus's own journey to become himself. He had fulfilled a number of his callings, but he still had to be the Saviour of the world. And while the cup would have tasted bitter at the time, oh how sweet it tastes for us today. And so God does not take the cup away. That night, Peter and the other disciples saw their hopes and dreams die, but God could see the resurrection that was coming and that many would be saved because Jesus stepped up and faced the darkness head-on.

God knows that life does not end with that cup, even though for us sometimes it feels like it does.

Peter though couldn't see this, and so he reacted as most of us do: he resisted. Malchus played the role of waiter, and Peter showed his displeasure with his service by slicing off his ear—*I said a glass of red, not a glass of death!*

Jesus cautioned him, 'Put your sword away! Shall I not drink the cup the Father has given me?'

When the cup is set before us, we can resist like Peter, or we can trust God like Jesus. When we resist, we usually end up hurting the world around us, whereas when we trust God, we end up healing it.

I must hasten to add that God doesn't send these cups to us. He's not out there looking to inflict pain on his children. What he does do is give us the grace and strength to deal with the brokenness of the world that we come into contact with, rather than hide us from it. He gives us the power to shine in the midst of darkness, rather than shield us from it.

Jesus drank a cup full of the world's brokenness, and it did not destroy him. Instead he became our light, one that even the darkness of death cannot snuff out. And in the same way, as we drink our cups, God will empower us so that we may be a light for others.

God may not take difficult journeys away from us, but if we, like Joseph, will cling to rather than resist him, we will find that what the world meant for harm, he has turned it for our good.

He doesn't send the darkness our way, but as we confront it, we make the world and ourselves better as a result. And so God's plan to restore the world to goodness, a plan borne out of love, is fulfilled.

But there is more.

God does not leave us to face the darkness of the world alone. The same strength that was available to Jesus, the strength that equipped him to face all he had to that night, is available to us as well. And Jesus has promised to be with us always, even to the ends of the earth. God is not indifferent to our struggle. He recognises that life can be scary, and that is why the most repeated command in the Bible is 'Do not be afraid.'

Throughout the Bible he comforts us with words like these from Isaiah: 'For I am the Lord your God who takes hold of your right hand and says to you, Do not fear; I will help you' (Isaiah 41:13).

God assures us of his presence with us and assures us that he will drink that cup alongside us and face the dark moments by our side. He also encourages us by revealing how the story ends. As Jesus said to his disciples, 'I have told you these things, so that in me you may have peace. In this world you will have trouble. But take heart! I have overcome the world' (John 16:33).

In other words, Jesus has the final say on how our journey ends, and he's told us what kind of light we are. Like him, we are the light that the darkness cannot overcome. It will not break us. Because of Jesus, and because our God never sleeps, this journey ends well for us. It will end well when Jesus returns to fully complete the restoration of the world, and it ends well for us now as we live through it.

And that is the good thing: the cup is not a never-ending one; it ends. As David said in Psalm 30:5, 'Weeping may endure for a night, but joy comes in the morning.'

So if your cup is bitter right now, take heart; your Saviour is with you and will not let the darkness overcome you. Very soon that cup will be empty, and the cup of transformation will taste oh so sweet in your mouth and in the mouths of those whom your journey has restored. So have faith and trust God; your morning beckons.

Jesus set the trail for us. He did not shy away from becoming himself because the road got tough. But he understands how difficult the road can be. He understands our Garden of Gethsemane, and he understands our cross. Even he gave that cry that we all have uttered: 'My God, my God, why have you forsaken me?'

He knows what it is like to feel forsaken. That is why he assures us that we are not alone. He knows what it is like to be drained of all strength. That is why he promises to be our source of strength, so that even when we are weak, we are strong. He knows how it feels to be afraid, and so he assures us of his help.

We can press forward in faith because Jesus is not only with us but also understands what it's like to be us.

> Do not fear, for I have redeemed you; I have summoned you by name; you are mine.
> When you pass through the waters, I will be with you;
> And when you pass through the rivers, they will not sweep over you.
> When you walk through the fire, you will not be burned; the flames will not set you ablaze.
> For I am the Lord your God, the Holy One of Israel, your Saviour.
> —Isaiah 43:1–3

15

Church Walls and Roosters

(Luke 22:54–62)

Perspective is a funny thing in that it is usually shaped by the environment we find ourselves in. The way we see life and respond to certain situations is often dictated by the environment that surrounds us at any given point in time. Take Peter for example. Before the events of Luke 22:54–62, where his famed denial takes place, his whole perspective on life was shaped by being around Jesus. It gave him great courage, as evidenced by his attempt to fight off all who had come to arrest his Lord. It gave him great faith. Of all the disciples, he was the only one who attempted walking on water. And it gave him a voice (some would say too much of one); he was always willing to speak up for what he believed, whether it was who Jesus was or what Jesus should and shouldn't be doing. He was a man who stood up for his convictions. And one of those convictions was that he would follow Jesus no matter what, even at the cost of his own life.

But now, after Jesus is seized and arrested, Peter follows from a distance.

Do you know what that feels like, to follow Jesus, but from a distance?

We, like Peter, find ourselves tossed between two frames of mind, the one that follows closely and the one that follows from afar because it doesn't cost us anything. And those two mindsets are often determined by the environment we're in. Say, for example, it's a Sunday morning and we're gathered in a church building with other Christians. Everything in that environment is geared towards keeping our eyes on Jesus. The choir are singing about Jesus, and the walls are decorated with pictures, paintings, and messages that point towards him as well. The pews are littered with Bibles and hymn books (cue thoughts about Jesus), and the pulpit usually has something symbolic and gigantic: a supersize Bible, a cross, or something else that points our focus again to—you guessed it—Jesus. And then when the leader steps up to speak—well, you'd hope he or she is talking about Jesus as well.

In that environment, it's easier to keep our eyes on Jesus and to see all things through the lens of his presence with us. Yes, we can still be distracted, but if we come into the building with the right attitude, chances are we'll end up with the right focus. Like Peter, we find that we grow in courage, faith, and conviction during the time we spend within those walls. Our ears are listening for just one voice, and whatever it is we're going through, we begin to believe in the power of God again. We are prepared to take on any opposition, walk on water, and stand up for what we believe in. We will follow Jesus no matter the cost, and when we sing, 'The cross before me, the world behind me', we are not messing about. We mean business.

But then life happens.

We leave the church doors and walk into the big bold world, and here is where our dilemma begins. Because while the church building is set up to focus our attention on the author and finisher of our faith, the world is set up to focus our gaze on something much different—self.

The messages we find around us are all about looking after number one. It is in everything we see and everything we hear, and it is constant. Messages like 'You're worth it,' 'You know you want to,' and 'Get yours' constantly fill our heads and cloud our judgement. It should be no surprise, really, as this is the world Adam and Eve signed up to inhabit when they disobeyed God in the Garden of Eden.

In that moment, they swapped a world where God was the focus for one where self was the focus. And that burden still carries on today.

It is difficult, perhaps impossible, to be disciples of Jesus when we are driven by an environment that is so geared towards focusing on self. This is why we find ourselves, like Peter, following from a distance and perhaps denying who we are in the crunch moments of our journey.

Peter denies Jesus three times. Similarly, there are usually three ways in which the noise of our environment influences our perspective on life. They are calls for self-advancement, self-gratification, and self-preservation.

Let's tackle the call for self-advancement first. This is a desire to promote ourselves and our interests above all else. It is one of the things that we're driven to, a desire for glory and recognition. For Peter, in that moment, it was simply that he wanted a seat at the fire. It was a privileged position that gave him a great view of what was happening with Jesus. It was in his best interests to maintain that position. At least that's what he thought. He felt strongly enough about it to be concerned that admitting to being a disciple of Jesus would mean that he'd have to give it up. And he really didn't want to give it up.

To admit that he was a disciple of Jesus may have also brought rejection from those around him. He would not have been welcome in their company. They may even have laughed at and mocked him: 'Isn't that your "Lord" being arrested like a common thug? We thought you said he was the Messiah?'

And so Peter declined to own up to who he was, preferring to keep his place at the fire instead.

I wonder what seats you don't want to give up.

Sometimes owning up to who we are in Jesus inevitably means giving something up, something that we may have considered of high value. One of these things is our quest for glory and recognition from others — recognition that is manifest by an invitation to take a seat at the fire.

Giving this up is tough because that seat is very desirable, and perhaps our pride is too strong. But we find that when we are sitting there, in that relationship, setting, or position, we are not thinking or acting like disciples of Jesus. Our focus is only on ourselves and how we can get ahead. We are thinking in terms of our own glory and our personal interests, with no thoughts about being light and salt or pouring out our lives for others. Our only thoughts are about our next glory shot or a dogged determination to keep our place. We're more likely to be marking out territories than shining light on them.

This is what the world around us promotes after all: blow your trumpet, toot your horn, protect your territory. And so we act like the environment tells us to. The odd rude joke to keep us in favour, the single-minded drive to get to the top, an inconsiderate attitude towards others, and on and on we go. In the end, our determination to seek after self-promotion leaves us with a life that is too busy and preoccupied with keeping our esteemed seat at the fire, and therefore we become unavailable and unapproachable to everyone else. We surrender, albeit unconsciously, to a motto that says 'Do what it takes to get what you want, irrespective of who is left behind, even if that person is God himself.'

And then we hear the voice that asks us the question 'Aren't you with Jesus?'

But we want to conquer the world. And this seat gives us the platform to do just that. It connects us with the right people, and it positions us in the right places. Then the voice says, 'What will it profit a man to gain the whole world but lose his soul?' If we were to gain the world but in the process forget who we are, have we really gained anything?

Again the question: 'Aren't you with Jesus?'

Then there is that old beast called self-gratification, giving in to our desires, whatever they may be. This is the voice that says, 'Go on, you know you want to.'

The fire is nice, warm, and desirable. It looks like it will make us feel good, if we could just have it.

'Have it then,' the voice says to us.

And, oh, we want to. Nothing could satisfy us like that fire could. We feel awfully cold, and it looks brilliantly warm. And so we edge closer. And the closer we get to the fire, the farther away we move from Jesus. The more we see the fire, the less we see our Saviour.

And then we hear the voice: 'Aren't you one of his? Don't you belong to Jesus?'

Images of the pleasures of this world, of sex, power, and other indulgence, flood our eyes on a daily basis. And with each flood, the subliminal message goes out: 'Go for it. It will make you happy!' If only temptation weren't oh so tempting. The fire feels good the closer we get, and so we pursue it. But you know what else fire does? It burns. And though we know this— we've heard it within the church walls, about the perils of life focused on the fire, and we've believed it—we can't seem to pull ourselves away from worshipping at its altar. Saying no to the flesh is never easy, especially when we are surrounded by a noise that tells us to say yes. It is a noise that encourages us to give the body what it wants.

This reminds me of a story I heard when I was young about a greedy little boy who was never satisfied. He would scream at his parents over and over again, with words that came to exasperate them: 'Give me food. I'm hungry!'

His parents would feed him with all they could find, but every single time after he had eaten what was brought to him, he would kick off again: 'Give me food. I'm hungry!'

The flesh is like that, constantly shouting out for more food. But like the boy in the story, it is never satisfied. No matter how many times we indulge the flesh, it never gets full. Instead it edges us closer and closer to the fire, until we get completely burnt.

Again, God calls us away from a life spent lusting after the fire: 'Why spend money on what is not bread, and your labour on what doesn't satisfy? Listen, listen to me, and eat what is good, and you will delight in the richest of fare' (Isaiah 55:2).

It is only in God that we truly find the satisfaction we're searching for. It is a truth we know well, but once we are out in the jungle of the world, how easily it is forgotten. There it is replaced with different 'truths' that tell us we need something else, 'truths' that our flesh is more than willing to get on board with. And so suddenly all our money and labour is invested into what does not satisfy.

And then the question comes to us again: 'Aren't you one of his?'

Then there is self-preservation, a basic human instinct to protect ourselves, to be on the defensive, especially when we feel threatened. This was probably Peter's biggest concern as he sat by the fire. Just a while back he had been willing to fight a group of armed men; now he was afraid of a small mob. The difference? His environment. Earlier on, he had Jesus with him, and now he just had the dark night skies. And so when he felt threatened, he lied to protect himself, a situation I suspect we all know too well.

When we feel threatened in any way, shape, or form, our basic lioness instinct kicks in, and it usually doesn't go through the filter of discipleship. Instead we lash out, we hold grudges, or like Peter we tell lies. Whether they are white lies or rainbow-coloured ones, lies are often told out of a desire to protect ourselves. And self-preservation means that rather than exposing our lights so they can shine, we keep them hidden.

Jesus asks us to turn the other cheek when we're struck. In other words, if you put yourself out there and you get hurt, put yourself out there again. Many times we go with the opposite theory. When we are struck on one cheek, we never show our cheeks again. We don't go back to church or to leadership; we don't make ourselves available or accessible; we don't give of our gifts or allow vulnerability.

Self-preservation: 'Defend yourself! Watch your back! Fight your corner!'

It is the message of the world, but Jesus's message is different. It tells us to keep our eyes on the kingdom and promises that God will keep his eyes on us. It tells us to fight for the kingdom because God is fighting for us.

And again the voice: 'Surely you're with Jesus!'

Would Peter have come to any harm if he had owned up to being with Jesus? I don't think he would have. Why? Well, because Jesus had promised to build the church with Peter as its leader, and Jesus never lies. So no matter the plan of the enemy, no matter the mob, they couldn't have hurt him, because God would have honoured his promise over Peter's life.

David understood this. When living as a fugitive in the wilderness, an opportunity was presented to him to kill Saul. I once wrote a fictional novel based on this story, and one of the people who reviewed it thought it was completely unrealistic. Why would David, given the opportunity to kill this man who had chased and hunted him down with no justification, pass up on it? The world cannot understand this logic, but David did.

David understood that it was God's responsibility to protect him, and God doesn't need a helping hand, especially when it involves doing something contrary to his will for our lives. The God who promised to put David on the throne was capable of doing it; the God who anointed Peter as leader of the church was able to bring it to pass. And us? The God who has promised to protect and care for us is more than able to do so.

Again the question: 'Come on, you're surely with him?'

But Peter denies Jesus, as we often do, and then the rooster crows. Interestingly it is at this precise moment that Peter catches Jesus's eyes again. And isn't that so true?

We always catch his eye after the rooster crows, after we've given into self-advancement, self-preservation, or gratification, after we've given in to the desire to serve ourselves and found that it did not satisfy, it did not advance, and it did not preserve. It is then that we catch his eye. And, like Peter, we find that the guilt and shame sets in.

If only we could have caught his eye at the beginning.

The good news is that we can. An environment centred on focusing on Jesus can be fostered outside the church walls as well. We can build habits and disciplines into our lives that remind us of the truths we hold dear and that point our eyes back to the Lord, who loves us the most. We can recreate the environment that equips and empowers us to follow Jesus wherever we find ourselves.

We do this by following God's advice in Isaiah 55 and eating what is good—a healthy spiritual diet—starting with breakfast, the most important meal of the day. It is important to create space at the beginning of the day to focus our eyes on Jesus, to start the day in the way we hope to live it. We don't have to awake before the crack of dawn as Jesus did, but we should take a moment to acknowledge his presence with us and our commitment to following him. This goes a long way as we journey through the day.

It doesn't have to be a three-hour prayer-a-thon or an in-depth meditation into the book of Leviticus, as long as it is meaningful and sincere. As long as it is the real us meeting with the real God. As any good dietitian would tell you, if you have a good healthy breakfast, you are less likely to snack on things during the day. Once we fill up on time with God, the distractions of the world are less likely to get us to snack on them. Our tummies are already full.

But we should never downplay the importance of a good lunch. Set aside time to feast—on a book that helps focus your attention on God or a song that does the same. Feast on the God-given gifts and talents in your possession, and use them to bring life to your world. Shine, and in so doing become yourself. Join a small group and feast on the knowledge and experiences of others, while sharing your own story for them to feast on.

In other words, spend time dealing with your spiritual hunger, or else you'll end up entangled with your fleshly hunger.

And at the end of the day, reflect with God as you would with someone you are in a relationship with. Reflect on the day. Thank him for what went well. Ascertain where you could have done better. Do this not to beat yourself up, but to receive his grace and be better prepared for tomorrow.

And when grace is offered—as it always will be—accept it and rest in it.

And as we persevere with this spiritual diet, as we invest in building Jesus into every facet of our lives, we will find it easier to see his gaze at any given moment. The voice and the question 'Aren't you with Jesus?' will not be a reminder or something that accuses; it will be the driver for our lives. Because the more we keep our eyes on Jesus, the less interesting the fire appears.

Our prayer every day should be to find our Savour's eyes. And God gives us this promise: 'Then you will call upon me and come and pray to me, and I will hear you. You will seek me and find me, when you seek me with all your heart. I will be found by you, declares the Lord' (Jeremiah 29:12–14).

So we don't need to wait for the rooster's crow before we go searching for Jesus. We can see him and take him with us wherever we go. Our Saviour is not confined to church walls. Below is a poem I wrote a while back about Peter's rooster equipment, as you meditate on his journey hopefully you find the spark you need to be triumphant in yours.

Three Crows

Crow 1

My words don't match my actions,

And my acts don't match the words I mention.

I told my Lord I'd follow,

But now out here my words feel hollow.

Frozen by fear and the hate that surrounds me,

Frozen by the voice of doubt that confounds me,

I find that I'm not able,

Even though I said I was next to him at the table.

Crow 2

My heart harbours desires,

Though not the kind that light up righteous fires.

I told my Lord I was ready.

Now I'm out on the road and my feet ain't steady.

Pulled by the lies and pulled by the distraction.

Can't stop my lips from making the retraction.

I said I'd put him first,

But now I realise I love me the best.

Crow 3

My hands need holding.

I thought I was strong, but look, now I'm folding

Under all the pressure,

Like I've lost my head and I've lost my measure.

I thought I was solid, but look at me denying.

Thought I was the rock, but look, now I'm crying.

I said, 'For you I'll die,'

But I've messed up so bad, I can't look you in the eye.

Crow 1

He said, 'Do you love me?'

I said, 'Lord, I do, and you know I'm sorry

That sometimes I keep failing

And that my life doesn't match the words that I'm saying.

I see the storm, and I hear my fears calling,

So I need your help to stop me from falling.'

He said, 'My words will hold you

And into a son and a warrior mould you.'

Crow 2

'Do you love me?'

I said, 'Lord, I do, but I don't think I'm ready.

I want to give you my heart,

But there's a part of me that won't let me do that.

Too many times I find I'm distracted

With the wrong things and get too excited.'

He said, 'My grace I give you,

And it'll build you up so the world can't deceive you.'

Crow 3

'Do you love me?'

My heart was broken, and I felt uneasy.

I said, 'Come on, Master.

You know everything, so you know my answer.

I know that I'm weak and that sometimes I struggle,

But that doesn't change the truth that I love you.'

He said, 'My son, I'll guide you.

And wherever you go, I'll be right beside you.'

16

Plot Twists and Tombstones

(John 20:1–10)

One of my favourite things about watching a movie or television series is a good plot twist. I especially love it when I think I've figured out where the story is going, only for a plot twist to come round and slap me in the face. I am a right sucker for those kind of storylines.

I was watching a particular box set recently (I won't name the show so as to avoid spoilers), and it looked like the story had come to an end. It was the season finale. The killer had been exposed and found guilty in court, and all that seemed to be left to do was to play the closing credits. But the end credits didn't come. The story kept going on, one scene after another. The writer in me wondered what the point was. Why hadn't the episode finished? Why were things being dragged out? I kept watching, and then right at the end, the unexpected happened and threw the whole story out of sync. It was the mother of all plot twists. I loved it!

Peter experienced a plot twist of his own at a time when he assumed the story had ended. Jesus had been taken forcefully from him and the other apostles, tried in a sham trial, and sentenced to death on the cross. And then the unthinkable happened: Jesus died. He was gone. Right until the moment Jesus heaved his last breath, Peter must have harboured some form of hope that Jesus would find a way out of this mess. He must have harboured some sort of hope that justice would prevail, that the truth would come out, or that some sort of miracle would take place. But then the news filtered in that Jesus was dead. Peter's hope, the whole point of his life, was lying in a tomb, lifeless. Making matters worse was the realisation that his last interaction with Jesus was to deny him. That was the last impression he had made on his Lord. Talk about an unsatisfactory ending.

Still an ending it was. At least that was how it must have felt to Peter and the other disciples. All that was left was for the ending credits to begin to roll, but then the story carried on.

Peter was in hiding, along with the other disciples, when Mary showed up at their doorstep with alarming news. She'd been to the tomb, but Jesus's body was not there. He'd been taken, and they didn't know where to. Their chief suspects in the case of the missing cadaver were without doubt the Pharisees, but what could they have wanted with the body of Christ?

Peter and John ran down to the tomb (and John made sure to point out that he'd beaten Peter in that race), and saw for themselves that Mary's words were true. Peter walked in and examined the crime scene. Before joining Jesus's movement, he had been a fisherman by trade, and now something sure smelt fishy. The strips of linen and the cloth Jesus had been wrapped in were still there, but there was no Jesus.

The story wasn't ending, and the closing credits weren't rolling. There was a plot twist coming.

Even then, Peter thought that this was it as far as plot twists go. The Pharisees had shown up and stolen Jesus's body. To what end he wasn't sure. All this was, was an unsatisfactory ending, and so he and John went home and continued as they were. In verse nine, John is candid in his admission that they still didn't understand that Jesus had to rise from the dead. As far as they were concerned, this story ended at the tomb. Opened or closed, with or without the dead body of Jesus, that was that.

God had something else in mind.

The Bible is full of different characters who had their own tombstone experiences, who came across a point in their journeys that should have marked the end of their stories, hopes, and dreams. Daniel was thrown into the lions' den; Shadrach, Meshach, and Abednego, into a fiery furnace; and Joseph, into prison. David was exiled from Israel, as Moses was from Egypt; the Israelites were trapped between the Red Sea and the bloodthirsty Egyptians, and Sarah was barren. In every one of these scenarios, the story looked over—and for all intents and purposes, the stories should have been over—but what all these people came to learn is that the tomb is not the end but, rather, is the beginning of something new, something better than we could ask for or imagine.

I don't know where you are presently, whether you feel like you've been thrown into the lions' den or into a fiery furnace. Maybe you feel like a heart without a home or a rebel without a cause, stuck in a wilderness or in a job you never saw yourself doing. Maybe you feel trapped between the Red Sea and bloodthirsty Egyptian soldiers, or perhaps there are areas in your life that feel barren and unfruitful.

Or maybe, like Peter, you're staring at a tomb that represents the death of a dream, relationship, or loved one. Whatever the case, the story doesn't end here. The end credits are not about to roll, and there is no gigantic THE END sign about to come up. It is only the beginning.

The ultimate plot twist is about to take place.

One thing I've learnt about God is that even when we cannot see a way, God sees several billion ways. Even when it looks for all intents and purposes like we are finished, God is still capable of turning things around, because even in the most grave-like of situations, Jesus is still Lord. So we need not despair about the tomb or the fiery furnace, because as intimidating and soul destroying as they may seem, we are not alone. We have God with us. And because we have him with us, we will be fine.

Deeper into the chapter, from verse 19, the disciples were hiding from the Jewish leaders in a locked room. As far as they were concerned, these guys had just killed an innocent man and stolen his naked corpse. There was no telling what kind of sinister madness they were up to or capable of. But right there, even though the doors were bolted firm, Jesus appeared in their midst.

And that's one of the beautiful things about Jesus: he can always reach us, and he will always find us. It doesn't matter whether we are hiding in our fears or sadness, whether we feel trapped, or who is trying to hurt us; wherever we are, Jesus will find us, will reach out to us, and most importantly will do life with us. David puts it this way in Psalm 139:11–12: 'If I say; Surely the darkness will hide me and the light become night around me, even the darkness will not be dark to you; the night will shine like the day, for darkness is as light to you.'

In other words, no situation is too dark for God's light to pierce through and save us. Peter had just denied Jesus, and the other disciples had abandoned him in his time of need. But it did not stop Jesus from appearing to them and bringing peace and a new beginning to their lives. No situation is so bleak or too far gone that God cannot turn it around. For God, it does not matter whether it's night or day, whether it's dark or bright; he is still God, and he is still capable.

We often see God from the viewpoint of our own human limitations. This is why when things get bleak, we expect the end credits to follow soon after. But God has given us his guarantee through Jesus that he will take care of us, that he will carry our burdens, and that he will lead us on the best path for our lives. And as Numbers 23:19 puts it, 'God is not human, that he should lie, not a human being, that he should change his mind. Does he speak and then not act? Does he promise and not fulfil?'

These were words I was confronted with as I stared at my own tomb, where my hopes and dreams had died a death. In these moments the enemy wants us to give up and throw in the towel. He tells us, 'It's the season finale. There's nothing to see here. It's done. All that's left is the end credits.'

In the box set I was referring to earlier, the movie didn't even end at the end credits. If I had switched off the TV the moment the end credits began to roll, I would have missed out on the biggest and best part of the story. And that is the enemy's plan, to get us to give up on a story that we are not even halfway through, to give in before the big moment in our journey occurs, to miss out on the miracle of resurrection.

Like Peter, we find it easy to give up and return to our locked rooms, to hide in our fears and our sadness. But if Peter had stuck around, he would have heard the angels say these words to him as they did to Mary: 'Why do you seek the living among the dead?'

And we will do well to hear those words as well. Sometimes we keep looking in the tomb, even when the story has moved on. Sometimes we allow ourselves to stay stuck in our grief and sadness and to wallow in our failures and disappointments, but God is doing something new in us, for us, and through us. The tomb is no longer where it's at. The story has moved on, and it's moved on to a better place.

The disciples were stuck pondering how things had come to this, how Jesus had been captured and killed, and the consequences it had for them. Mary was stuck wondering whether the gardener had been a coconspirator, complicit in the move of Jesus's body to a different location, and Peter was stuck in his guilt.

But the story had moved on to somewhere spectacular. And the disciples would see it too once they stopped looking for life in the wrong places, once they stopped looking in the tomb and began looking for Jesus, once they understood that their Saviour was not dead but alive and that their Lord was the Lord of the living, and so they had life as well.

The same is true for us. We cannot live life as though our Saviour is not risen. We cannot give in to fear and despair as though Jesus does not exist, as though he is not at God's right hand interceding on our behalf. Our Jesus is Lord of the living, and our faith in him means we have life. It is the promise we were given in his Word. And God says this about his Word: 'As the rain and the snow come down from heaven and do not return to it without watering the earth and making it bud and flourish, so that it yields seed for the sower and bread for the eater, so is my word that goes out from my mouth: It will not return to me empty, but will accomplish what I desire and achieve the purpose for which I sent it.'

So when we are confronted with the tomb, we can rest assured that the story does not end there. It is not a reason to despair but, rather, is the start of a new and excellent journey with Jesus. We need only to have faith and look away from the tomb and into his eyes. Because there's a big and beautiful plot twist on its way.

And it's in your favour.

17

Back to the Waters

(John 21:1–14)

How do you deal with disappointment? How do you deal with a pain that just won't go away? This is where we find Peter in the final chapter of John's Gospel. Jesus has appeared to the disciples twice since his resurrection, and while it must have filled Peter's heart with great joy, it probably also made him feel even more aware of his inadequacy. On those two occasions Jesus appeared to his disciples, it must have felt for Peter like there was a big elephant in the room, namely his denial of the man he had promised to follow no matter what.

He felt more like Peter the fisherman than Peter the rock, and so he got up and returned to the waters.

Remember at the start, when we first meet Peter, that this is where he is. And Jesus gives him an option: continue fishing or come and join me to do great things in the world. But when Peter fails, when the doubts about his capability return, he goes back to what he knows. He returns to the familiar space of the sea. The overconfident, cocky disciple who was very sure of himself is gone, and instead we are reacquainted with Peter the vulnerable fisherman he was at the beginning of his journey.

He returns to the waters because this is where he would get his affirmation from before Jesus showed up on the scene. Before Jesus, he had a very low opinion of himself. In Luke 5:8, when Peter is made aware that he is in the presence of someone special, he says to Jesus, 'Go away from me, Lord; I am a sinful man!'

Perhaps the water was the only place he felt useful. When he sailed on that boat and caught some fish, it made him feel that at least he was good at something. It gave him a feeling of exhilaration, however temporary. And so in his moment of self-doubt, he returned there. It's interesting that he didn't pray. Jesus had taught them how to pray, given them a template for prayer, and modelled a life of prayer regularly to the disciples, particularly to Peter.

Yet in his disappointment, Peter didn't turn to prayer; he turned to the waters. That's strange, or is it?

In our journey as disciples, we too will also face our own moments of disappointment, failure, and self-doubt. In these moments, where do we turn? When prayer doesn't seem to have worked, or when God seems silent, where do we go?

The spiritual superstars amongst us may stay fixed in prayer and faith, but for the rest of us, we often go back to the waters. We often return to where our affirmation previously came from, the thing or person that made us feel good before Jesus.

In those moments we want something tangible, and we are not content to wait on God or to believe that this is just a 'tomb' moment and resurrection is around the corner. When we are down in the dumps and struggling, we want something tangible to latch on to.

As did the Israelites all those years ago.

In Exodus 32 we read the story of how the Israelites got tired of waiting for Moses to come down from the mountain, so they asked his brother Aaron to make them a different god, one that was more tangible and also agreeable to their desires. Aaron rolled up his sleeves and delivered the golden calf.

What's your golden calf? What do you turn to when you get tired of waiting on God?

Peter returns to the waters in search of affirmation, but as they had done so many times before, the waters let him down. It's like fast food; the idea of it is more satisfying than actually eating it. My sons get so excited by the thought of a Happy Meal, but once it's bought, they hardly ever finish it. The thought of it is far more exciting than its actual taste. It is the same with the waters. The idea of it always trumps the actual experience. It looks way better than it tastes.

Peter returns to the waters in search of affirmation and ends up frustrated. He and his fellow fishermen tried, but that night they caught nothing. It is the same for us when we turn elsewhere for affirmation, when we go back to the things that we believe used to make us 'feel good'. The problem is that our mind plays tricks on us. We forget there was a reason we left these waters in the first place. We forget the damage they did and the completely unsatisfying feeling they gave us. So we return, but it only adds to the frustration, and we end up feeling worse off than we felt before we'd set out.

If you've ever felt disappointment, failure, or self-doubt, then perhaps you know exactly what I'm talking about. The journey will not always be smooth, and there will be times when we let ourselves and others down. There will be times when we deny Jesus, and there will be times when things don't pan out quite as we'd hoped they would. In these moments, the temptation to return to what we know or used to know is great. The desire for an instant high or a quick win, however temporary, is strong, but we must hold fast and wait on Jesus.

Because the waters never affirm or satisfy. Like with fast food, the idea of them seems scrumptious, but their actual taste is horrible, bland, and unsatisfying. In truth the waters leave us worse off than where we were before. Again the words from Isaiah 55 come to mind: 'Why spend money on what is not bread, and your labour on what does not satisfy?'

We are better off following the advice Jesus gives: 'Pray and never give up.'

As Peter and his mates engage in their futile pursuit of fish, Jesus shows up on the shore. And it is his interaction with Peter again that brings affirmation to Peter's life. When he hears Jesus's voice and follows his instruction, he finds the affirmation he was searching for. He feels capable again. He feels useful. What happens here, as the disciples follow a stranger's voice and pull in a large bounty of fish, is reminiscent of one of Peter's early encounters with Jesus. John, who is with him on the boat, puts two and two together.

'It is the Lord,' he says.

The wonderful thing about our leader is that he doesn't shy away from meeting us wherever we are, even if that is the waters. Even when we fail, even when we return to the mess though we should know better, if we would only look up and listen, we will hear our Saviour's voice calling out to us, 'Friends, haven't you any fish?'

In other words, did you not find what you were looking for out there? I know from experience, the answer is usually a big fat no. But Jesus doesn't give us the 'I told you so' treatment; instead he tells us what to do: 'Throw your net on the right side.'

Stop looking in the wrong places for affirmation, stop looking for the living amongst the dead, and search for me instead. Cast your eyes to the right place. And isn't that message so true?

When Peter realises it is Jesus, he jumps out of the boat and races out of the waters towards him. As the fish fill up his net, he realises that all he really wanted was to be with Jesus. The affirmation he needed was one that not even a million bursting nets could give him. Only Jesus had the answers he was searching for.

Are we still looking to bursting nets for validation?

Are we seeking the bursting net of a healthy bank balance or the bursting net of pleasure, status, and glory? Are our lives still geared towards finding affirmation this way? The idea that we are someone when we achieve this or own that is an easy trap to fall into. But Peter learnt that his validation lay at the feet of Jesus. He was someone because Jesus loved him; he mattered because Jesus chose him. There were many fishermen in Israel, probably many who were better at what they did, but it was him whom Jesus chose.

The same is true for us. You are someone because Jesus loves you. Of all the people in the world who bear your name, he chose you, and he set you apart for a journey as his disciple. We don't need bursting nets, and we don't need the waters. All we need is Jesus. And he is always there.

Sometimes he may not show up how we want him to, but he always shows up, just as he did for Peter.

The disciples had no control over when Jesus appeared to them, or in what form he appeared, but Jesus always appeared. He showed up when he was needed. And when he returned to heaven, he made sure we had his presence with us, in the person of the Holy Spirit.

So, Peter got out of the waters and found that Jesus was waiting for him. There was a fire, and there was already fish and bread. All this time, it wasn't Peter waiting for Jesus's next appearance, it was Jesus waiting for Peter to show up. And the same is often true for us. Those moments when we think we are waiting for God and that he is being so distant and silent—the truth is that he is often the one being kept waiting. He is at the fire, waiting to cater to our need, but we have gone off to the waters in search of alternative care.

The waters don't just frustrate us, they also serve to distract us from the presence of Jesus.

While the disciples' attention was on catching fish, they did not notice the man waiting on the shore or the fire that was lit for them. And while we are pursuing other sources of pleasure and affirmation, we miss out on God's voice and presence; we miss out on his provision.

So, have you got any fish? Return from the waters; there's nothing for you there. Jesus is waiting on the shore. Go and sit with him instead. He is all you'll ever need.

18

Red or Blue Pill, Take 2

(John 21:15–19)

Not too long ago, Peter was sitting in front of a fire, in what proved to be the scene of his greatest disappointment and failure, a place where he'd lost everything. Before that fire, all had seemed well. Peter knew who he was and where his life was heading. He was sure he had it all figured out. He was a disciple of Jesus, and alongside his Lord, he was going to establish a new kingdom. They were going to do it together. That kingdom was going to be the start of a new revolution. They were going to do great things together, and the gates of hell did not stand a chance against them. Everything was so clear. Peter had dismissed Jesus's suggestions of death, refusing to entertain the thought that anything would happen to the man he believed to be Israel's Messiah. He refuted even more the idea that he himself would turn his back on Jesus. He could never do that; he intended to follow Jesus to the very end, to stand by him, fight for him, and if necessary, die with him.

Then came that night by the fire.

Everything seemed to go downhill from there. Jesus had been arrested and was being tried, and Peter was sitting at a distance observing events.

I suspect what followed had kept him up at night since that day. Three times he was offered the opportunity to stand up for the man he claimed to love, to profess what he believed, and three times he declined; three times he failed. As if that weren't bad enough, in the mistrial of a lifetime, Jesus was found guilty, sentenced to death, and brutally murdered, and Peter was forced to live through his worst nightmare. What an awful night that was.

Now, days later, Peter is sitting at another fire, this time with Jesus. Jesus has been resurrected. Apparently he'd been telling them all along that this was going to happen. Apparently the whole Bible spoke about his death and resurrection; the disciples must have missed Torah classes that day. This is Jesus's third appearance since his resurrection. On the previous two occasions, as far as we know, the issue of Peter's denial had not been addressed. And then from nowhere, Jesus asks him the question: 'Simon son of John, do you love me more than these?'

You could have heard a pin drop. Imagine being one of the other disciples in that moment. It would have felt super awkward. *Oh dear,* they must have thought. *Peter is going to get it now. Jesus didn't just call him by his Hebrew name; he's even getting his dad involved.*

You really know your goose is cooked when a loved one double-names you when asking a question. But that is not where Jesus is going with this.

In the previous chapter, we saw Peter returning to the waters, his previous source of affirmation. Peter is like Cypher, the character from *The Matrix* who becomes disillusioned with life in Zion and decides that he'd rather return to life as it was before Morpheus. In the same way, the young disciple, feeling incompetent and unworthy, decides to pick up his nets again. But as Peter sits down with Jesus at the fire, Jesus asks where his loyalty lies. What does Peter want more?

Is he happy to go back to what he was before, or does he want to continue believing in Jesus? Is he still interested in knowing just how far the rabbit hole goes?

Jesus comes to us with the same question. He has done the same with me so many times. 'ND, do you love me more than these? Your dreams, your status, your wealth, yourself; do you love me more than these?' It is like when God asks Abraham to give him Isaac, or when Jesus asks the young man to give up his wealth. It is a question that goes to the core of the matter and deals with the alternative 'Saviour' in our lives, asking us whom we really trust for salvation.

Do you want to get affirmation from the waters, or am I enough?

It's some question. There is a song we used to sing growing up. It goes along the lines of, 'I am satisfied with Jesus, but is he satisfied with me?' I think the reality is the other way round. Jesus is satisfied with us. He wouldn't swap us for anyone else in the same way that we wouldn't swap our children, no matter how badly they may behave. We may want them to do better, but they will always be the ones we choose.

But are we satisfied with Jesus? Or do we want a golden calf that is tangible and agreeable to our desires? Or maybe a Baal, because almost everyone else is worshipping Baal? Is Christ enough? This is the question Jesus poses to Peter—and to us.

In Peter's case, the answer is affirmative: 'Yes, Lord, you know that I love you.'

Peter chooses Jesus, and Jesus replies, 'Feed my lambs.'

Jesus in one of his teachings referred to himself as the Good Shepherd and to his disciples as his sheep. As he reinstates Peter here, he gives him a responsibility: give my lambs what they need in order to become sheep.

Throughout Peter's journey, while he may have seen himself as a brave raging bull, in reality he was just a lamb being fed. This is where we all are when we first come into discipleship; we are but lambs that need feeding. Jesus has nurtured Peter and fed him, and as Peter takes his final face time lesson on earth, Jesus is saying to him, 'As I have fed you, feed those whom you will disciple.'

It is a calling that is not just for Peter. Every one of us has the Great Commission as our mission, a calling to go out and make disciples. And in doing this, Jesus expects us to disciple others in the way we were discipled by him: in love and grace. He expects us to take the lessons we have learnt from our own journey and use them to help and encourage others. Inspired by his own journey with Jesus, Peter writes these words in a letter to the churches in Rome: 'To the elders among you, I appeal as a fellow elder and a witness of Christ's sufferings who also will share in the glory to be revealed: Be shepherds of God's flock that is under your care, watching over them—not because you must, but because you are willing, as God wants you to be; not pursuing dishonest gain, but eager to serve; not lording it over those entrusted to you, but being examples to the flock' (1 Peter 5:1–3).

In other words, disciple as you were discipled.

But Jesus is not content to leave things there. Having dealt with the issue of Peter's alternative saviour, he goes on to deal with another pressing issue hanging over his disciple, namely his loss of faith, the reason he returned to the waters in the first place.

When Jesus asks Peter the second and third time, 'Simon son of John, do you love me?' he is doing this not for his own benefit, but for Peter's. Jesus is well aware of where Peter's heart is; it is Peter who has doubts. Many questions probably surround Peter's head following the denial:

- Why did I fail?
- What is the guarantee I won't fail again?

- How could someone like me with such a public fall ever be fit to lead?
- How does Jesus feel about my failure?

Peter had begun to define himself by his failure, and Jesus was not having any of that. Even today, some of us define Peter by that failure. And it's not just him to whom we give that treatment; we are accustomed to defining people by their failures. Peter is the disciple who denied Jesus, Thomas is the one who doubted, David is the king who bedded another man's wife, and Solomon is his womanising son. On and on, we define our world and those in it by its failures, and so it is no surprise that when we fall, we do the same to ourselves.

But God doesn't work that way. He does not see us through the lens of failure, and he doesn't want us to see ourselves through that lens either.

What definitions come to your mind when you think of your life? Do you define yourself by a failed relationship, job, or dream? That's exactly where Peter was. So when Jesus says to him, 'Simon son of John, do you love me?' he is helping Peter rediscover who he is again, the one definition that truly matters: he loves and is loved by Jesus. He is his disciple, one who will follow him, one who will become himself.

And though Peter may have stopped believing that, Jesus never did.

Jesus's belief in Peter was unwavering. Come old and new fire, come declarations of love or denial of the Saviour, Jesus still believed in Peter. Peter never lost his credibility in Jesus's eyes, even if he may have in his own. The same is true for us.

Jesus believes in you when you're thriving and when you're struggling. He believes in you when you're conniving Jacob, and he believes in you when you're covenanted Israel. He believes in you when you are barren Abram and when you are fruitful Abraham. He believes in you when you are hateful Saul and when you are loving Paul. And he believes in you when you are doubting Simon or the solid Peter. His love is not conditional, and his grace is not earned.

Both are freely given.

Sometimes we stop believing in ourselves, and we get disillusioned with the journey we're on. Like Cypher in *The Matrix*, we want out; and even when we don't want out, we don't quite know if we've got it in us to stay in. It is in these moments that Jesus shows up to light our fire again. David put it this way: 'You Lord, keep my lamp burning; my God turns my darkness into light' (Psalm 18:28).

Jesus shows up on the scene and begins to work through the darkness. And most times, he does this through questions. He prompts us in this way because there are things we need to see for ourselves, confessions we need to say with our own lips, and convictions we need to accept with our hearts. So he asks Peter, 'Do you love me?' Like he had asked him before, 'Who do you say I am?'

Throughout scripture God calls out to his people with questions. From Adam and Eve to Moses, from Elijah to Ezekiel, and then to Peter, and then with us.

In our moments of doubt, Jesus comes to us in the same way. He opens our eyes to see that the truth has not changed. Life may change, situations and circumstances may change, and the story may change, but the truth does not change. And the truth is, we belong to him, and that is all we need. He will never abandon us, and he will never stop believing in us. And even when we get lost, he will always come looking for us.

Peter answers the questions, and he does not get reprimanded by Jesus. He simply gets refocused. He is reminded and affirmed as Jesus reveals his identity to him again: You're the guy who takes care of my sheep. You're the guy who feeds them.

In other words Jesus is saying to him, *You're not the guy who denied me; that's not you.* And Jesus does the same for us. He refocuses our minds and hearts on who we are, taking our eyes back to the right place. We have a tendency to focus on our mistakes and failures, to allow ourselves to be dragged down by them. Sometimes we obsess on them so much that we become that person. We become the personification of that failure. Jesus encourages us to move on from our mistakes, and he does so in the same way he did at the beginning: by saying, 'Follow me!'

Again the red pill and blue pill are placed before us. We can take the blue and wallow in the regrets of our failures, or we can take the red pill and follow Jesus into life.

Over to you, Disciple.

The Crow or the Fire?

Do you hear the crow?

Sometimes it's all I hear

Like a repeated jab, a recurring nightmare.

It calls out my name and calls out my shame.

It rolls up its sleeves in contempt and takes aim,

Saying, 'Oi, Peter, Mr Rock, Mr "Pillar" of the church,

Or is it killer of the church?

So you cast out demons and walked on water,

And then you go deny your Master?

Mate, you're no rock; you're banter,

Melting at every temptation, throwing shade at your
salvation.

Build the church on you? What a notion.

You wince at the words of a servant girl,

And you want to go out and save the world?

I'll tell you this much, and you know it's true:

You'll never love him more than you love you.'

Yes, I hear the crow,

But I stopped listening to it long ago.

I choose instead to listen to the fire,

As did Moses and Elijah,

For it holds the voice of my Messiah.

You see, the crow may be harsh and outspoken

And point out where I'm weak and broken,

But in the fire lies the voice of redemption

With words of grace and affirmation,

Saying, 'Peter, I choose you.

Peter, I send you.

Peter, I honour and defend you.

Come hot or cold, come scared or bold,

When the wine is new or battered old,

You're still my plan. You're still my choice.

Your vessel still carries my voice.

The crow may say you don't belong, but Peter, I am never wrong.

And where you are weak, my grace is strong.'

So the crow can bark, and bleat, and scatter,

Cos the words in the fire, that's all that matters.

The crow or the fire?

I choose to listen to the fire. What about you?

19

Conclusion—the Others

(John 21:20–22)

Unlike the last time Peter had his red or blue pill moment, he doesn't grab for the red pill. He is hesitant. As relayed in John 21:20, he turns and looks in John's direction and asks the question, 'Lord, what about him?'

In this moment when Jesus is calling Peter to follow him, when he is not just reinstating him but also reiterating that he believes in him, why is Peter worried about John's journey? How does what is going on in John's life have any bearing on Peter's particular journey?

It's probably for the same reason we worry about the journey of others, the age-old practice of comparing our insides to someone else's outsides.

And we all do it in one context or another. I have the tendency to look at someone with a similar gifting or at a similar phase of life to mine and examine what they have achieved in comparison. I usually only compare myself to those doing much better, and when I don't measure up favourably, I use it as a rod to thrash myself with.

Too many times in our journey we take this approach. We look at that other Christian who seems to have it all figured out, or that other church, or that relationship, and we despair at our inadequacies in comparison. The thing is, wherever it hurts on the inside, the Devil is only too happy to offer us a point of comparison, to create a mirage for us to beat ourselves with, anything that takes our focus off following Jesus and sends us onto a path of self-pity and, in some cases, resentment.

Peter looks over at John, and in his eyes, he doesn't measure up. John didn't deny Jesus at the fire, and while he ran away and hid, John was at the foot of the cross at the time of Jesus's death, looking out for his mother. Add to that the undoubted closeness between Jesus and John, and it is easy to see why Peter was distracted. Suddenly it wasn't enough for Peter to accept Jesus's calling over his life; he wanted to know John's as well. He wanted to compare both to see just how high in esteem Jesus held him. Because compared to John right now, he didn't feel adequate.

'What about him?' 'What's your plan for him?' 'What are you doing with him?'

We often have this same busybody syndrome. We glance sideways and wonder, *What about them? They're doing well, aren't they?* It's an easy formula that slows us down or stops us in our tracks. A glance towards the others, those who seem to be doing better and coping better than we are. Not only is comparing our insides to the outsides of others a dangerous path, it is also an inaccurate one.

If you only knew how many people compare their insides to your outsides and feel inadequate.

Jesus's words to us, when we stumble into this mindset, would be the same as the ones he spoke to Peter: 'Do not concern yourself with the others; you must follow me.'

At the end of the day, Jesus wants you, the real and complete you, with all your mistakes, questions, and flaws. It is you he chose, chased, and died for, and he has no regrets. He's not interested in you as a version of someone else, but the original you. Jesus didn't want Peter to be more like John, any more than he wants you to be more like Mr X or Miss Y. He didn't want Peter's ministry to be carried out a bit more like John would deliver his; he wanted Peter to be Peter, and he wants you to be you.

When I was just a little boy, there was another boy in my class who was, to my mind, quite amazing. He was the most intelligent boy in our year, acing every class and winning every prize. I would often look at him and make comparisons, and I didn't measure up very well. It wasn't long before I began to harbour the thought that perhaps God had sold my parents short. He should have given them that boy as a son, not me. I was convinced that the other boy was more deserving of the life I had. Even from that tender age I had started to compare my insides to someone else's outsides. This feeling of unworthiness ate me up inside, especially on the days we picked up our report cards and that boy had come out top of the class again.

I still don't know how my mother picked up on the fact that I felt that way, but mothers just seem to have this supernatural radar. One day, right out of the blue, she sat me down and reassured me with these words: 'If I had to choose between you and him, I would choose you every single time.'

She must have seen the surprise in my little face, just as I saw the love and sincerity in her eyes. Those words transformed my life. I stopped comparing myself to anyone, and it didn't matter what that boy did or achieved. And powered on by that affirmation, I went from average student to one of the best in my year as well. It was a complete transformation, and all it took was a change of focus.

Jesus does the same for us.

In our weakest and darkest moments, he says to us, 'I choose you every single time.' The Bible lets us know that Jesus died for us when we were at our worst. He gave us his greatest act of love at a time when we were not thriving, at a time when we were at our lowest. He chose us even before we knew how to stand on our feet. He believes in us, and he trusts us. And he says, 'It is you I want with me on this journey.'

This is what Jesus says to Peter: don't worry about what is going on for others; it is you I want with me on this journey. You follow me—focus on the truth that I love you, I have chosen you, and I believe in you.

Even when we don't believe in ourselves, he believes in us. And it is not just lip service. He trusts us with gifts and abilities, he trusts us with relationships and communities, and mostly he trusts us with his name. He gives us his name to carry with us. Whether we are thriving or weak, we carry the name 'disciple of Jesus'. Sometimes we are too ashamed to carry our own name, but God is never ashamed to give us his. He is never ashamed to declare that we belong to him, no matter what.

We may feel inadequate. We may feel like we're not good enough. But that is not an opinion that Jesus shares. Besides, it is by his strength that we can do all things. Our success on the road is dependent not on what we are capable of but on the limitless power of the living God, who walks alongside us.

I am convinced that if Jesus had to do it all over again, he would still choose you, he would still chase you, and he would still die for you. Because God is not man, he doesn't change his mind about you.

When Jesus responds to Peter with the words 'You must follow me!' I don't believe it is an order. Jesus doesn't give orders where discipleship is concerned; he gives invitations. And what he is saying to Peter is, 'You must accept this invitation.'

It is a plea for our own good. You must accept this invitation. It is a journey you don't want to miss. Jesus makes the same call to us in the moments when we are unsure and weary: 'You must follow me!' It is a journey we need, one that is created solely for the purpose of bringing life to us.

Sometimes we compare the season we are in to someone else's. Theirs looks all bright and beautiful, while ours in comparison looks dark and stormy. But every season counts. If you look at the life of David, for example, you'll see that he went through different seasons in his own journey, but every one of them was relevant. The throne of Israel was a great end point, if you like, but God was at work in his life at every different stage. God was present in his journey as shepherd boy, choirboy, and giant-slaying boy. God was present when David was leader of Israel's army and when he was leader of a group of fugitives. God was there in the wilderness, and he was there in the palace. And through all those seasons, God's presence meant that David thrived and shone, and that through him God impacted lives then and for all time.

Each season was just as important as the next one, and God's ability to work wonders in David's life was not limited by David's location or phase in life. David sometimes was tempted to look at the journey of others, especially when he was stuck in the wilderness, but he learnt to keep his focus on God instead. In Psalm 37:7 he shares these words: 'Be still before the Lord and wait patiently for him; do not fret when people succeed in their ways, when they carry out their wicked schemes.'

David understood that every season was relevant. Without the previous seasons, he would not have been the king that he was. And more importantly, in every season God was at work in his life. We do not need to be seated on a throne to experience the power and blessing of God in our lives. And we do not need a throne before we can shine. Even before the throne, God was doing great things in David's life, as he did with Joseph when he was in prison, with Moses in the wilderness, and Jesus on the cross.

There is no season too dark that God cannot shine his light in and through it.

Once we recognise that every season we are in is relevant, that whether we are in prison or the wilderness we are still able to shine like the sun, we will stop making comparisons and focus on the grace that God gives for every journey we embark on.

There is nothing to be gained from comparing our journey with others'. All it leads to is a sense of inadequacy, a feeling of self-doubt, and a loss of faith. Jesus implores Peter to stay focused on him. He did the same to me. I referenced what he was doing in someone else's journey compared to mine, and he gave me the exact same words: 'What is it to you? You must follow me!'

And so I did, and I have written this book in obedience to him and in response to that invitation. Because I came to realise that what happens in someone else's story does not make mine any more or any less valid or relevant in the work that God is doing. Our value comes from the knowledge that God chose us for this particular journey, that he believes in us, and that he has chosen the path that suits us the best.

Jesus offers us the invitation to follow and keep our eyes on him. So do not worry about what is happening elsewhere. Trust in his unfailing love and his perfect work for and in you. Keep your eyes on the author and finisher of all you believe in.

When Joshua was about to lead the people of Israel, he had gigantic shoes to fill in the person of Moses. Most would feel completely inadequate compared to a man of Moses's stature, I definitely would. But as Joshua weighed up the huge challenge ahead of him, God encouraged him with these words: 'Have I not commanded you? Be strong and courageous. Do not be afraid; do not be discouraged, for the Lord your God will be with you wherever you go' (Joshua 1:19).

He encourages us in the same way. Sometimes the journey ahead may seem too daunting, the wilderness too vast, and the prison cell too empty. Sometimes the season we are in may seem dark or unending, but then God meets us with these words: 'Is it not I who has called you? Is it not I who chose you? Is it not I who believes in you? There is no reason to be afraid or feel discouraged. There is no reason to give up or feel like you are not good enough. You can face every journey with strength and courage, because I your Lord will be with you wherever you go.'

What great words.

There can be no greater honour than knowing the Lord and Creator of the universe wants to walk and work with you, that he loves your gifts, your story, and your you. Let these words transform your journey as they did the journeys of those who went before us. And let the understanding that God's presence is always with you, and is all you need, fill you with strength and courage, irrespective of the season you're in.

It doesn't matter what is happening elsewhere. It doesn't matter how nice things may appear in other journeys. You have an invitation from Jesus with your name on it, and this is an invitation you can't turn down, a journey you just have to go on. None of us can, especially because it's not a journey we have to do alone. We don't have to figure things out by ourselves or understand what each season means and how it links to the next one. All we need to do is to trust and follow him, to be still before him and wait for his guidance.

And know this: as you go forward on the journey that you are on, and as you march on from season to season, you have the backing and confidence of your Saviour.

So be strong and courageous—you are his treasure, you are his masterpiece, you are his disciple.